Our Pirate War:

How the U.S. and its Navy defeated pirate bands off of North Africa (1783-1807)

Philip Blake

ISBN 978-0-557-56328-9

Introduction

The infant American Republic moved into the 19th century fighting a long, unconventional war against pirate gangs which supported themselves preying on merchant shipping and global trade. Even prior to enactment of our Constitution, the U.S. faced the reality of 21 of its citizens being seized and held in Algiers as slaves for labor and ransom.

The money made in piracy and slave markets were economic mainstays of four quasi-states lined along the Mediterranean coast of North Africa. Their economies followed a pattern of piracy that dated back as far as Julius Caesar. Our founding fathers were confronted by extortionate threats from the nation's first days.

The first three presidential administrations encountered this hostility directly. George Washington launched the first plans for a Navy to defend American shipping against Barbary piracy. After succeeding Washington, John Adams pushed Congress to fund and authorize the U.S. Navy.

But the key American leader in this long war was Adams' political rival and successor: Thomas Jefferson. He had dealt with the issue as an American diplomat in Paris immediately after the American Revolution. Later, as the third President, Jefferson went on to direct the Navy's strategy. and the funding for the fleet. He selected the commodores who led the American fight against the pirates in the Mediterranean. And he sacked those naval commanders if they didn't perform. Edward Preble, the most notable Jefferson naval appointment, was responsible for setting early standards for the US Navy, which led to remarkable success. Many of Preble's precepts in leadership and principles of strategy survive until now.

The four quasi-states that harbored the pirates were under the umbrella of the Ottoman Empire. The strongest was Algiers. Morocco, with a coastline on both the Mediterranean and the Atlantic, made peace with the United States early in the struggle. Troubles flared on an off with Tunis over a 25 year period. The heaviest fighting during Jefferson's two Presidential terms was with Tripoli (now Libya).

All four of these governments supported the pirate forces that set out from their shores. Their economies relied heavily on the tribute the pirates forced from many European nations. They also relied on labor from enslaved merchant seamen and other slaves to do much of the heavy labor of their society.

The United States badly needed trade. The thirteen colonies were heavily in debt when the revolution ended and the nation needed a vigorous resumption of foreign trade in order to repay it. It also had a strong colonial heritage of favoring free trade and freedom of the seas.

The Barbary conflict represented the first sustained projection of American military power far from its own shores. In the process some strong precedents were set by Jefferson and his military and diplomatic leaders which would influence the country's similar ventures down through the years. In an environment where the great European powers had paid tribute to recover enslaved citizen and prevent piracy, the United States resisted paying ransom and tribute. (In turn, it was forced to do so. in some situations.)

This small but long war forced five American Presidents to consider when the United States should use force far from its shores, and when the use of an invasion force is warranted. Jefferson and Adams wrestled at length with the size and composition of the Navy. Jefferson and James Madison, his Secretary of State and successor as President, set precedents in how to blend the threat and use of military force with economic threats and diplomatic efforts. Jefferson had to decide how to deal with an American effort to replace a foreign leader with a rival more aligned with American interests. James Monroe, Madison's successor, brought these conflicts to a successful conclusion in 1815.

This book focuses on the work of these early Presidents and their cabinets and advisors directing military and diplomatic efforts thousands of miles distant in a time of difficult and slow communications.

As important, this is a story or remarkable and courageous Americans, proud of their new nation, who lived extraordinary adventures. Their actions led to their names being memorialized as the names of American cities and US Navy vessels down to this day:. Some of those names are Decatur, Bainbridge, Eaton, Porter and Preble. This is their story and that of the deliberations and leadership of the President who oversaw much of their great adventure: Thomas Jefferson.

Chapter I

Before Thomas Jefferson sailed back to the United States from diplomatic duty in Europe on the cutter_Clermont in October, 1789, a surprise already was awaiting him back home. His nomination as the first American Secretary of State by President George Washington had been ratified by Congress nearly two months earlier.

For Jefferson, the nomination was unexpected. In an age when the swiftest communication took weeks to cross the Atlantic, Washington's nomination of Jefferson to direct American foreign policy arrived as a great surprise. Jefferson suspected he might be asked by the first American President to return to Paris as Minister to France.

And the new US Constitution assigned the Secretary of State the leadership role in the federal government's heightened powers over the new nation's foreign policy. The first crisis that Jefferson would face in his new role was one he had dealt with during his five years of work in Paris: protecting American merchant sailors from the Barbary pirates and securing their release when they were captured. Jefferson left Europe with this work unfinished, as 21 Americans remained in a slave prison in Algiers after four years captivity.

Jefferson did not suspect that the specter of Mediterranean pirates would pursue him through his service to the new nation, (especially eight years hence during a first term as President). The scourge of piracy caused Jefferson to project the power --- especially the naval power --- of the new nation to distant shores for the first time in its history.

These fledgling steps in extending American power by Jefferson and his colleagues --- particularly Washington and John Adams --- echo to this day through two centuries of American foreign policy

Jefferson, who was 46 years old, delayed accepting his new appointment for more than two months. He was uncertain of his ambition for such a prominent post. Also, the cabinet position bore responsibility for all of the routine administrative functions of the newly formed U.S. government. Jefferson considered himself unsuited for this work and he was not at all interested in such an administrative role.

But the call of country coming through Washington, a uniquely revered leader, won out. Jefferson said he "bowed to the inevitable" and accepted Washington's appointment on Feb. 14, 1790.

When Jefferson arrived in the first national capital of New York on March 21, 1790, and reported to the President their agenda was topped by the 21 American merchant seamen held as slaves in Algiers.

The Barbary pirate states had preyed on European shipping for centuries, creating a complex and elaborate system of trading in humans to generate government revenues. Until the end of the American Revolution, ships of the American colonies were protected by British tribute payments to buy peace from the North African states. But soon after the signing of the Treaty of Versailles on September 3, 1783, the rulers of the four Barbary states caste avaricious eyes on the advance of American merchant vessels into the Mediterranean.

Their first capture of a United States vessel was deceptively simple for Americans to solve. In 1784, the *Betsey*, a brig from Boston bound for Tenerife (in the Canary Islands), was captured by a Moroccan corsair. Sidi Mahomet, the Moroccan Emperor, had a strong interest in trade and little reputation for cruelty. So he sought a treaty or pact of friendship with the new American government. In the meantime, he housed the American merchantmen relatively comfortably out of prison. The *Betsey* and her cargo were held safe awaiting emissaries from the new U.S. Congress. Six months later Spanish emissaries intervened on behalf of the U.S. government. The crew of the *Betsey* and the ship and its untouched cargo were released for $10,000 and the promise of a future treaty.

Soon afterward the three commissioners representing American interests in

Europe predicted attacks on American shipping from the far crueler and more powerful state of Algiers.

So Thomas Jefferson, John Adams and (for a few months before his return to Pennsylvania) Benjamin Franklin, began a remarkable dialogue about strategies and approaches to employ against the four piratical states of Algiers, Tunis, Tripoli and Morocco.

Within three months of the release of the Betsey and her crew, the strategic talk was no longer theoretical. In July, 1785, the American schooner *Maria,* near the end of a long Atlantic crossing to Portugal, was captured by an Algerian xebec. Less than one week later, the Boston schooner Dauphin was captured by Algerian pirates outside the straits of Gibraltar.

The cruelty leveled at the Maria's crew of six was quick and fierce. The corsair crew tore any wearable clothes and shoes from the bodies of the American sailors as they boarded the xebec as prisoners. They were then forced into the hold of the small Algerian vessel, where they found already 36 prisoners crammed together in the tiny vessel who had been taken in earlier raids. One prisoner reported a dark atmosphere of "heat, filth and stench.

The captives landed in Algiers several days later, after the winds allowed the small pirate craft to reenter the Mediterranean from the Atlantic. "Being private property" the captured sailors were "stripped of the remnants of … clothes which remained." This description comes from the captivity tale of James Cathcart, of the six-man crew of *Maria*. Cathcart said he was "furnished in lieu thereof with the remains of an old dirty shirt and brown white cloth trousers which were swarming with vermin which, with the crown of an old hat, composed the whole of my wardrobe."

Cathcart was skilled at seizing opportunity from grim circumstances and managed to rise through the elaborate system of "trusty" positions employed in the Barbary bagnios (slave prisons). By the end of his 11 year imprisonment, Cathcart owned a tavern catering to Christian slaves (a sole outpost of alcohol in this Muslim state) and had become the Dey's Private Secretary --- the highest slave position in the system.

Cathcart's imprisonment was unique, however. The many other European and Americans held captive in Algiers led lives of misery marked by scant filthy clothes, rotting food and ample religious hatred from their guards. "Which Christian dog, Infidel dog without faith, I will have you bastinadoed to death" was a guard's threat recorded by Cathcart in his journal.

Cathcart was subjected to the bastinado, the unique form of Barbary torture which was a brutal beating of the soles of the feet, after noticing a Portugese captive being beaten with sticks, causing him to roar "most tremendously".

"I asked his crime but received no answer before I was seized by four stout Moors who threw me down, pinioned my legs and arms and the same game was played on the soles of my feet to the tune of twenty-eight hard blows, which produced the most excruciating pain and left me with four toe nails less than before this game commenced.

All fourteen (prisoners) were served with the same manner, none were pardoned for age or infirmity, but old men of sixty and children of ten years of age received the bastinado without ever knowing what it was for."

Many of the prisoners died of the plague. However, death to these prisoners was not directly caused by their masters, whose economic system was dependent on the products of their labor while they were still in captivity, and later their ransom or sale as slaves. While severe cruelty was acceptable in Algiers, too harsh a cruelty worked against the slave owners' economic self-interest.

Cathcart's account guides us through the Algerian slave economy. He described easy work in gardens where fruit is grown for the Dey, his chamberlains and the grandee slave owners. In contrast, hundreds of Christian slaves were engaged in rock hauling for construction of the Algiers harbor "mole" (or breakwater) built with large rocks they hauled manually to the site.

"Figure to yourself above a thousand poor wretches, many of them half naked without hat or shoes, at work in the heat of the sun all day till four and sometimes till five or six o'clock on a summer day, carrying earth in a basket to the top of a high building, exposed to the heat and often blistered with the sun, chafed and scalded with the weight of their load, the perspiration flowing from them....."

And he listed their diet as follows:

"...on working days there is a mess of burgul boiled in the Marine; mixed with a quantity of butter worse than tallow ... it frequently happened they find rats, mice and other animals boiled in the burgul, which is by no means a pleasant addition to their mess; nevertheless I have seen many hundred during my captivity sit down to some buckets of this stuff, substitute a chip for a spoon and eat as voraciously as some of our epicures would turtle soup, terrapin or venison pastry."

The cruelty visited on the Americans in Algiers was in part a hostile reciprocity between Christian Europe and Muslim North Africa in existence for more than 1,000 years. The capture and use of slaves had been vital to the maritime world when galleys were propelled by oarsmen. As brutal as the conditions the Americans endured, they were less severe than those suffered by most galley slaves

With sail power ascendant, the need for slaves for propulsion had lessened. But the Christian faithful had not completely foresworn capturing slaves at sea in the Mediterranean, and revenge motivated some of the cruelty leveled by both sides. In fact, both the xebec

Captain who captured the *Maria* and Ibram Rais, the cruelest bagnio warden that Cathcart encountered, had been captives of Europeans.

Rais had recently returned from 14 years of captivity in Malta. As he ordered slaves into leg irons, he advised them: "...I will show you there how I was treated in Malta. Here, Sbirro (a guard), put leg irons on these gentlemen's legs.".

Shortly after the *Maria* crew arrived in Algiers, they were joined by the 15-man crew of the *Dauphin,* led by its captain, Richard O'Brien.

As word seeped slowly back to the United States of the capture and treatment of the Americans, public pressure grew on the U. S. Congress to take some action to secure their release.

The early American diplomatic corps in Europe of Franklin, Adams and Jefferson were brilliant, but the group represented an American government attempting to define very limited power available under the Articles of Confederation. As such, their diplomatic efforts were supported by little money, no force of arms and vague leadership and direction. Also, (as Jefferson would observe later regarding his appointment as Secretary of State) timeliness of communications was a real problem.

Before he headed back to Pennsylvania, Franklin prepared a first draft of a treaty that could be used with the Barbary states, based on intelligence he had garnered in Paris about existing treaties made by European powers. Jefferson and Adams worked on it individually from their respective bases in Paris and London. But in 1785 they began collaborating. The resulting dialogue was a kind of two person colloquium by two brilliant novices struggling to learn and practice the art of diplomacy.

The Barbary pirates and their enclaves on the coast of Africa took their name from the pair of Greek Barbarossa ("red beard") brothers who launched westward attacks along the North African coast in the early 16th century. The Eastern Mediterranean was a sea of Christian and Muslim conflict. The North African coast became fertile territory for the brothers to exploit after 1492, when Ferdinand and Isabella defeated the Spanish Moors and expelled them from the country. Thousands of embittered Moorish refugees, intent on revenge, crossed the Mediterranean and settled in North African coastal cities,.

About 1504, the Barbarossa brothers, Aruz and Khizt, sailed into Tunis on two "galleots" to begin to build their pirate enterprise. That the brothers came from

European backgrounds was not surprising. The Turks had been enticing or capturing and converting Europeans to their cause for decades. The Barbarossa brothers were born of such roots on the Greek Island of Lesbos.

Their father was believed to be a janissary. (Janissaries were typically Europeans who had been captured as children and converted to Muslim and the Ottoman cause.

Janissaries played important roles in the government and military, but never had the rights of Turks.) The Barbarossas' mother was the widow of a Greek Orthodox priest. The Turks particularly relied on capture or conversion in building a maritime force. Until the capture of Constantinople in 1453, they had no great port as an outlet to the sea for their growing empire, so a Navy had held no value.

The Barbarossa brother known as Aruj had been a galley slave on a ship operated

by the Knights of St. John. This experience of being whipped to work oars while chained naked on a slave galley ship doubtless fed the ferocity and cruelty he showed later when he was the captor.

Aruj and his brother, Kheir-ed-din, established a base in Tunis and began seizing Mediterranean trading vessels and their crews. Many victims came from Western Europe --- Spain and the city states of Italy, including from galleys owned by Pope Julius II.

The coast of North Africa held many perils, including poorly charted shallows and reefs and strong winds (which would later figure in the U.S. Navy's trials there).

These navigational and piloting hazards offered natural defenses from foreign adversaries to the pirates. Beginning with Aruj and Kheir-ed-din. The pirates had learned to navigate through them while operating along this coast,

In a series of raids in the early 16th century along the coast, the brothers moved Eastward through what is now Algeria. They attacked Spanish outposts like Bourgie and seized European ships of varying origin --- bringing their passengers and crew to the North African slave markets.

Aruj died in an attack by a Spanish force determined to blunt his looming domination of North Africa. The vigorous Barbarossa expansion did not falter though, as Kheir-ed-din succeeded him immediately and made contact with the Sublime Porte in Constantinople, thereby moving under the umbrella of the growing Turkish empire.

Kheir-ed-din's success in battling the Spaniards and Italians contrasted with the Turks' experience in the Eastern Mediterranean, so the Porte summoned him to Constantinople and quickly installed him as Admiral of the Ottoman Navy, which was in disarray.

The Barbarossa brothers and their followers spread the nautical skills and economic system of piracy throughout North Africa. One of Kheir-ed-din's key trusted subordinates took over Tripoli (which later would be the prime site of combat with the U.S.) five years after the second Barbarossa brother had died in his bed in Constantinople in 1546.

The prevalence of piracy as a long-standing practice throughout the Mediterranean is clear from the great historical figures who were touched by it in their lives in Southern Europe. Julius Caesar famously had been enslaved by pirates early in his military life. Nearly 30 years after Kheir-ed-din's death, the ship carrying Miguel Cervantes from Naples to Spain was seized by Barbary corsairs. Cervantes spent five years in an Algerian prison awaiting ransom from home. His experiences doubtless was the raw material for the "Captive's Tale" section of Don Quixote.

The lives, tactics and culture of the Barbary coast which would be faced by the American Navy at the beginning of the 19th century descended directly from the Barbarossa brothers.

Chapter II

American ships in the Mediterranean fell under the protective cover of the British fleet until the Revolution. Great Britain was the dominant maritime power there (since taking Gibraltar in 1707), but even the British made payments to the Barbary powers.

From the end of the American Revolution, British naval might and financial tribute no longer protected American trade or ships, which were vital to the colonial economy.

Reestablishing European trade was high on the list of assignments to the American diplomatic triumvirate in Europe when Jefferson arrived in Paris in 1784 (joining Franklin and Adams). The new country was heavily in debt and economically depressed from the war, so trade was a priority. The Mediterranean was important to American trade. Jefferson later estimated, in a report to Congress, that one sixth of the wheat and flour and one fourth of the fish exported by the colonies were directed toward the Mediterranean. The American merchant shipping force which operated in the Mediterranean consisted of roughly 100 vessels totaling 20,000 tons and employing 1,200 seamen. 1

Europe had adopted a pattern of tribute, ransom and personal bribes to officials and bureaucrats to maintain the safety of Mediterranean commerce. The leaders of the Barbary states were adept at manipulating the Europeans to maximize the take. They broke treaties over imagined slights and used a variety of deaths, cosmic events or changes of rulers as a pretext to demand more tribute and luxurious personal gifts.

Jefferson resisted adopting the practice of tribute from the start. In a letter to Adams, Jefferson wrote, "…I very early thought it would be best to effect a peace through the medium of war…".

He then listed his reasons, including: "1. Justice is in favor of this opinion. 2. Honor favors it. 3. It will procure us respect in Europe, and respect is a safe-guard to interest."

However, Jefferson's ability to avoid tribute and ransom was severely limited by his equivocal attitude toward building American military power, particularly the power of a Navy. This would also be the view of his political allies, and to the Republican party they founded together.

He expressed this internal conflict as the Revolution neared an end, writing in <u>Notes on Virginia</u>: "And perhaps, to remove as much as possible the occasions of making war, it might be better for us to abandon the ocean altogether, that being the element whereon we shall be principally exposed to jostle with other nations; to leave to others to bring what we shall want, and to carry what we can spare. This would make us invulnerable to Europe, by offering none of our property to their prize, and would turn all our citizens to cultivation of the earth; and, I repeat it again, cultivators of the earth are the most virtuous and independent citizens."

Jefferson and Adams began their diplomatic work and dialogue to free American captives and enable its trade and shipping in 1784. Throughout their dialogue on tactics and strategy ran the philosophical differences between Adams, the pragmatist who noted the new country's early inability to build a naval force, and Jefferson who was conflicted over the creation of such a force, but eager to use it.

The major powers of Europe were indifferent or hostile to the United States as an independent trading nation. Many European diplomats and merchants viewed the U.S. as an undeveloped but potentially strong competitor in trade and shipping.

However, the British (perhaps somewhat in reaction to their recent humbling in the Revolutionary War) played the most active role in encouraging undercutting of the Americans as they reentered the Mediterranean. Franklin, the senior U.S. official who had worked longest and closest with the British, said after the Revolution:

"I think it is not improbable that those Rovers may be privately encouraged by the English to fall upon us, to prevent our Interference in the Carrying Trade, for I have heard it is a Maxim among the Merchants, that, if *there were no Algiers, it would be worth England's while to build one.* I wonder, however, that the rest of Europe do not combine to destroy those Nests, and secure Commerce from their future Piracies."

Foreign Minister John Jay wrote Jefferson in 1786 that the European commercial states "never rejoice to see a rival at peace with these pirates." Indeed, English shipping interests were offered direct competitive advantage by the attacks on U.S. ships. After the attacks took full force, Lloyd's insurance rates for American bottoms were raised to ¼ of the value of their cargo, effectively removing them from the competitive battle for regional commercial shipping.

But a direct statement of official English support for the pirates came from a member of Parliament, Lord Sheffield, who wrote in 1783 that the newly freed American colonies represented no threat to England, "… except as to the carrying trade, the nursery of seamen, and this is in our power to prevent to a considerable degree." Sheffield then added, "…it will not be the interest of any of the great Maritime powers to protect them there from the Barbary states. If they know their interests, they will not encourage the Americans to be carriers. That the Barbary states are advantageous to the Maritime powers is certain."

England had developed strong relations with the Barbary regencies in the 1600's based on a shared antipathy to Spain, which had battled with the English Navy at sea, and with North African Moors on the Iberian peninsula. English historian Sir Godfrey Fisher marveled at the relationship in his book Barbary Legend: "I have found no evidence that between 1682 and 1830 any other country maintained relations with us so consistently correctly as the three regencies." (of Algiers, Tunis and Tripoli). The 18th century warm relationship between the British and Algiers was made clear in an exchange of letters between King George III and Algerian ruler Muhammad Pasha that established the Algerines would fulfill England's wishes "giving them priority over all nationalities."

Jefferson and Adams recognized their inexperience in diplomacy, and specifically in dealing with the Barbary states. Their acknowledgement of this showed in part in their seeking the counsel of an experienced (if short-lived) ally French Foreign Minister Comte de Vergennes, even before the Maria and Dauphin had fallen into Algerian hands.

Jefferson's solicitation of advice from Vergennes was subtler than the always direct Adams. Adams quizzed Vergennes thoroughly, about everything from the amount France paid the Barbary states to the future of a French Treaty with Algiers, which was soon to expire. Vergennes provided no information in response to these questions and generally was of little help.

However, he did offer some advice that likely shocked Adams, the diplomatic novice. When asked if the U.S. should invite the Emperor of Morocco to send an envoy to work on a treaty, Vergennes said no, explaining that the U.S. would be expected to pay all the expenses of the envoy's "voyages and journeys which would be much more costly than for Congress to send a Consul (to Morocco)." This foreshadowed an unbelievable litany of demands, threats and begging for money received from almost every official, (high or low) of the Barbary governments encountered by the Americans.

Jefferson and Adams were both puzzled by the willingness of all European nations to pay tribute to the Barbary states. While all of European shipping was prey to the piracy, the smaller states were far more vulnerable, lacking financial and naval strength. The Italian city states, Portugal, Denmark, Sweden and Malta were specifically targeted.

From this situation grew Jefferson's idea of a forming a coalition of states whose shipping was imperiled to strike back at the Barbary world. He worked on this throughout his service in Paris and for years thereafter.

In the summer of 1785, Congress authorized $80,000 to secure Peace with the four Barbary states of Morocco, Algiers, Tunis and Tripoli. Congress had dispatched Charles Lamb to Europe to work on the Barbary problem, but had provided Adams and Jefferson no clear direction on specifically how to utilize Lamb (whose presence they had not requested).

Any orders Lamb bore from Congress and even his whereabouts (as he made his way circuitously to meet the two American diplomats) were a mystery to both Adams and Jefferson.

Jefferson wrote Adams on June 22, 1785, "What is become of Mr. Lambe? I am uneasy at the delay of that business....". In August, Jefferson followed with a letter implying that he had previously received word of the two U.S. ships brought captive to Algiers the prior month. (Jefferson and Adams' correspondence were necessarily vague and sometimes in code as they discussed security matters with one another and colleagues in Washington.) He then referred to Lamb's mission:

"But unfortunately we know also that a particular person has been charged with instructions for us; these five months who neither comes nor writes to us. What are we to do?"

He then proposed substituting American Revolution Naval hero John Paul Jones for Lamb, knowing that Jones could gather military intelligence about Algiers for a later Naval mission that Jefferson envisioned, "An important object would be obtained by Capt. Jones's becoming acquainted with their parts, force, tactics, etc."

While they awaited Lamb, Jefferson offered Thomas Barclay, U.S. Consul General in Paris, for an assignment to open negotiations with the four Barbary states for a treaty with the United States. In September, Jefferson proposed that Barclay begin with Morocco. With access to both the Atlantic and the Mediterranean Morocco was viewed as strategically more important that the other three. Also, the Moroccan Emperor was viewed as friendlier to the new American nation than other Barbary leaders. Jefferson sent Adams draft instructions to be given Barclay for his assignment Also contained was the suggested split of the $80,000 in tribute authorized by Congress ($40,000 to Algiers, $20,000 to Morocco and the balance split between Tripoli and Tunis).

On September 19, the errant Lamb arrived in Paris bearing orders from Congress giving Jefferson and Adams authority to "treat" with the Barbary states. Jefferson adjusted on the fly, directing that Barclay go ahead to Morocco, and that Lamb travel to Algiers. In a letter written less than a week after Lamb's arrival, Jefferson laid out to Adams a plan, including ways to monitor the activities and financial dealings of Lamb, about whom both he and Jefferson had clear (and as later learned warranted) misgivings. These included dispatching a clerk with Lamb "...who, in case he thought anything was going amiss, might give us information," and asking Adams to serve as Lamb's banker, authorizing any drafts on behalf of the United States.

Jefferson also forwarded more solid and specific knowledge of the fate of the Americans held captive in Algiers, in the form of a letter from a captive, Captain Richard O'Brien, which Jefferson said gave "...powerful motives for commencing by some means or other, the treaty with Algiers more immediately than would be done if left on Mr. Barclay. You will perceive by that two of our vessels with their crew and cargoes have been carried into that port. What is to be done as to those poor people?"

The New England merchant Lamb was unsuccessful in Algiers. Jefferson learned this in May, 1786, and began ending Lamb's mission which was almost as hard as launching it had been. Lamb made his way slowly back toward Paris, ending up in Alicant, which he refused to leave while he sought further payment for expenses. Despite the precautions placed over funds he could access, he had managed to deplete all funds available.

Jefferson and Adams were both embarrassed with Lamb's role, but the former far more so. Seven months after they received word of

Lamb's performance in Algiers, Adams felt compelled to reassure Jefferson:

"If Congress thought the original appointment censurable they had reason. But you and I were not censurable. We found him ready appoint to our hands. I never saw him nor heard of him. ---He ever was and still is as indifferent to me, as a Mohawk Indian. But as he came from Congress with their Dispatches of such importance, I supposed it was expected we should appoint him. ---There is no harm done."

Even the captives who observed him in Algiers found Lamb an unsuitable envoy on the United States' behalf, with O'Brien writing Jefferson of their surprise that Congress would send "such a man to negotiate so important an affair ...where it required the most able Statesman and Politician."

But neither man was really surprised by Lamb's lack of success, as Adams had received word from Algiers that the captors expected ransom of $6,000 for a master, $4,000 for each mate and $1,500 for each sailor --- far more than Congress was likely to authorize.

In contrast, Barclay's mission was a singular success. For a one-time payment of $25,000, he gained peace and the promise of friendly trading relations with Morocco's Emperor.

Barclay offered to continue on to Algiers, Tunis and Tripoli to recreate this success, which Jefferson quickly endorsed. But after an exchange of letters with his partner in London, he deferred to Adams who had written "...I confess I cannot see any advantage in it, but in the contrary several disadvantages."

Adams' view of the practicality of diplomacy to deal with the Barbary threat had been changed by remarkable face to face meetings that he alone and then with Jefferson conducted with the Tripolitan Envoy Abdurrahman in London while they awaited the outcome of the Lamb and Barclay missions:

"It would be imprudent in us, as it appears to me to incurr any further Expence, by sending to Constantinople, or to Algiers, Tunis or Tripoli. It will be only so much cash thrown away, and worse, because it will increase the appetite of these Barbarians already too greedy."

Adams had called on Abdurrahman in February, 1786, after learning that he was miffed that the American had not visited to pay his respects. Adams later recounted to Jefferson his remarkable first meeting, which was conducted in a smattering of Italian phrases and "Lingua Franca", the mix of European and African languages often spoken in the Mediterranean region.

Abdurrahman pronounced his liking for American tobacco and then a servant who brought "...two Pipes ready filled and lighted. The longest was offered me....It is long since I took a Pipe but as it would be unpardonable to be wanting in Politeness in so ceremonious an Interview, I took the Pipe with great Complacency, placed the Bowl upon the Carpet, for the stem was fit for a Walking Cane, and I believe more than two Yards in length, and Smoaked in awful Pomp, reciprocating Whiff for Whiff, with his excellency..."

After Adams followed Abdurrahman's lead through coffee and snuff "with such Exactness and Solemnity" one of Aburrahman's functionaries cried out "in Extacy, Monsieur 'vous etes un Turk'."

The Tripolitan went on to express his express his admiration for America, but announce that Tripoli was at war with Adams' country. "Sorry to hear that," Adams responded. "(I) had not heard of any war with Tripoli," adding that neither country had encountered any hostile contact with the other.

Abdurrahman acknowledged that, but said Tripoli required a treaty for there to be peace and suggested they meet to pursue such an accord the next day. Adams promised to think about it.

He wrote Jefferson seeking his reaction and counsel, concluding, "The Relation of my Visit is to be sure very inconsistent with the dignity of your Character and mine, but the ridicule of it was real and the drollery inevitable. How can we preserve our dignity in negotiating with Such Nations?"

In subsequent meetings in February, Adams became more optimistic the dialogue might be fruitful and that Abdurrahman might even negotiate treaties with the other three Barbary states. On Feb. 21 he urgently invited Jefferson to London to join him in the negotiations. Jefferson arrived on March 11 and stayed for nearly two months. The talks did not require that long, but the visit provided an opportunity for Jefferson to tour and for the two men to discuss their work with European nations and to renew their bond of friendship.

After the failure of the Lamb mission to Algiers and the abortive negotiation with Abdurrahman, Jefferson began a dialogue with Adams weighing the Americans' alternatives. Both men related the need to confront Barbary aggression, knowing their new nation's severe need for trade to pay back debts left from the Revolution. Both men tallied the costs of negotiation and naval power against the projected benefits from trade and shipping.

Adams envisioned the price to buy peace as 500,000 pounds sterling. He estimated the value of the loss of all Mediterranean trade, half of the Atlantic trade with Portugal and Spain, and insurance increases of 6 to 8 % of all exports as exceeding 500,000 pounds. And he foresaw the cost of a naval cruise against Barbary as also costing more than the 500,000 price to buy peace.

Jefferson's ledger looked considerably different. Telling Adams that he preferred war as a means of obtaining peace, Jefferson cited justice, honor, and increased respect in Europe as his prime reasons. But he also provided a tally which projected an annual cost of 45,000 pounds for a 150 gun fleet. Of this cost, Jefferson allocated half to a Mediterranean assault. He pointed to the need for naval forces elsewhere as well.

But he also foresaw a trans-Atlantic alliance beginning with Portugal and Naples and then "...many, if not most, of the powers of Europe (except France, England, Holland and Spain) would sooner or later enter into this confederacy, for the sake of having their peace with the piratical states guarantied by the whole."

The pair also discussed the level of alliance of the Barbary states to one another and to the Ottoman Empire as well. They quickly concluded that attempting to negotiate with the Ottoman Emperor for the whole Mediterranean bore no advantage, in part based on Vergennes advice recounted by Jefferson, "(Vergennes) says that those people indeed acknowledge a kind of vassalage to the Porte and avail themselves of it when there is anything to be claimed; but regard it not at all when it subjects them to duty; that money and fear are the only agents at Algiers."

In fact, the relations between the four Barbary states and the Turkish empire had been loose and ill-defined for centuries. The ruler of Algiers, the most powerful regency, was called "monarchical", "perilous" and "burdensome" by historian Joseph Morgan. Noting the Dey's absolute power, Morgan added, "frequently occur strange revolutions, procured by the inconstancy of a fierce and insolent militia, who oftentimes wither grow inraged at the Rigor, or abuse the Lenity wherewith they are governed...." Between 1700-1736 six Deys ruled and only one's reign ended voluntarily.

In the long run, both extortion money, and armed Naval and Marine force were used. Short term, however, the pragmatic Adams was correct in his judgment that "...neither Force nor Money will be applied. Our states are so backward that they will do nothing for some years….". This would come only after the greater federal power of the Constitution and diplomatic and military leadership from the executive branch it established.

Adams' conclusion was that the American public had decided to "…give up all Ideas of Navigation and naval Power, and lay themselves at the Mercy of Foreigners…. We must submit for your plan of fighting will be no more adopted than mine of negotiating."

By the spring of 1787, Jefferson concluded that a direct path to freeing the hostage in Algiers was likely impossible. But he thought there may be possibilities by adding deception to the mix.

He learned of a religious order, the Mathurins, who worked on behalf of Christian slaves in the North African slave markets. He thought that such a group, appearing to operate independent of the United States, might interest the Algerines in releasing their American prisoners for a reasonable price.

To do this, Jefferson and other Americans had to feign disinterest in the imprisonment of their countrymen. As Jefferson biographer Dumas Malone noted, "The only perceptible effect of this maneuver was to distress the captives and cause them to blame him…"

The lack of support from Congress operating under the Articles of Confederation after the Revolution was nearly inevitable. It had no money, heavy debts and limited sources of revenue. It had disbanded or sold off the limited Navy that had assembled to fight for independence. So neither paying extortion or fighting the extortionists was practical.

In fact, some have suspected that Jay and others back in the U.S. were hopeful that the dilemma in attempting to free the captives illustrated the severe weakness of the new American nation under this form of government and would help them push for more centralized federal power. That effort to create more central government power would later succeed with the ratification of the Constitution.

So the stronger federal government under George Washington that Jefferson was about to join as Secretary of State in 1790 was one that he had helped to create, even if he harbored real doubts about the wisdom of strengthening federal power.

Chapter III

The new Secretary of State delayed for three months reporting in New York for service with the cabinet of the first American President while he dealt with his own problems that had arisen in the years that he worked in Paris. When he did arrive in New York, he found the new State Department employed a five person staff to manage the nation's foreign affairs while also needing to fulfill the general administrative functions of the government.

The Barbary prisoners were an immediate priority. Congress and the President requested a plan from him for freeing the prisoners in Algiers and responding to the Barbary threat.

Jefferson's attitudes had not changed since he assumed his new post. He looked forward to having an influence over the government's strategy. "I am clear that nothing but a perpetual cruise against them, or at least for eight months of the year, and for several years, can put an end to their piracies," he wrote Edward Rutledge, "and I believe that a confederacy of the nations not in treaty with them can be effected, so as to make that perpetual cruise, or our share of it, a very light thing, as soon as we shall (have) money to answer even a light thing; and I am in hopes this may shortly be the case."

Jefferson's formal proposal urging the use of force against the Barbary states was also delivered to Congress in July, 1790. He argued that subduing the Mediterranean threat had merit as he already had recited to Adams, "...the cruise... may become a very lucrative and advantageous object for the United States."

He recommended that the US retaliation against the pirates commence with "a great blow" delivered by a 40 gun frigate and "two others of lesser force" constructed to be "the fastest sailors that they might on occasion avoid a too unequal combat."

The goals for this cruise, as outlined in Jefferson's proposal, were to achieve peace with all the Barbary states without payment of tribute, gain return of all captives and recompense for captured ships and cargo, and to "compel the Regencies of Barbary to respect for the time to come the flag of the United States."

Near the end of the year Jefferson completed his formal reports to Congress on the subject with his report on Mediterranean trade and a report on the status of the captured Americans in Algiers. Jefferson's reports were received by a Senate committee headed by John Langdon. The committee responded favorably to the proposal but quickly referenced "the state of public finances" as a significant obstacle.

Jefferson had deliberately delayed his report on the prisoners out of a desire not to reveal the efforts of the Mathurins in their behalf. But by the time he reported to Congress it had become clear to him that the Mathurin effort would fail, as the religious group was being disbanded by the French Revolution. He later described the effort vaguely to a colleague, noting that the US had hidden its support for the prisoners by funneling it through the Spanish consul in Algiers and added, "A certainty now that our measures for their redemption will not succeed renders it unnecessary for us to be so reserved on the subject and to continue to wear the appearance of neglecting them."

The prisoners were understandably alarmed by this apparent disinterest. They petitioned their government in March, 1792, noting aid received earlier, and then adding, "...but those supplies (of money) have Ceased for a Considerable time during which we have been reduced to the Utmost distress... dependent on the charity of Transient people."

With the Mathurin effort a failure, it was apparent a new tact was needed. Jefferson decided to employ Revolutionary War naval hero John Paul Jones as an emissary to Algiers. Jones had urged Jefferson on several occasions to act against the pirates. Now Jefferson noted two side benefits of employing the old war hero. His military accomplishments could serve as a none-to-subtle reinforcement to the Algerian Dey that the alternative to a peaceful settlement could be costly. At the same time Jones could reconnoiter Algiers for intelligence in case he or his countrymen later would need to use force to free the prisoners. For now, Jones was authorized to spend up to $50,000 to secure peace with Algiers and ransom the prisoners.

Jones' orders discussed another feature of prior negotiations that had been hidden, including from Jefferson. John Lamb, apparently at the suggestion of Congressmen who had assigned him to Jefferson and Adams in Europe, discussed naval stores or a frigate as a method of payment to Algiers in lieu of cash. This proposal to trade arms for peace was reported back to Jefferson much later from a variety of sources, including correspondence from prisoner Richard O'Brien in Algiers.

Consideration of providing arms to Algiers (while contemplating an "alliance of the threatened" with Naples and Portugal) was bluntly rejected by Jefferson when he learned of the idea after the fact. He wrote to Jones, "… we will not furnish them with naval stores, because we think it not right to furnish them means which we know they will employ to do wrong.…"

But Jefferson didn't realize that Jones had become critically ill. Jones' orders (mailed in cipher to Paris, where he had been living) arrived there in July, 1792, two days after his death. Then amazingly, the man Jefferson selected as Jones' replacement, Thomas Barclay, also died while his orders were en route.

Jefferson's direct involvement in the Mediterranean world was about to be interrupted while still unresolved. Jefferson had been a reluctant member of Washington's cabinet, only acceding to the President's appointment from a deep sense of loyalty. But he found the position and his work in the cabinet deeply unsatisfying. A central feature of this dissatisfaction was Jefferson's ongoing open feud with Treasury Secretary Alexander Hamilton about political philosophy

Washington was bothered enough by this to write both men in August, 1792 urging them to quell their personal attacks on one another. Jefferson had been hinting to Washington for months that he was looking forward to retiring. (At the same time, he urged Washington to seek reelection, for the good of the infant republic). In September, 1792, he submitted his letter of resignation.

Washington eventually sent David Humphreys to Algiers. In the meantime, however, the demands for ransom had increased. The Algerians had received payments of $1,200 to $1,500 per prisoner from the Russians and the Spaniards. Slave trading and holding were at the center of the Algerine economy and their macabre "inventory", had decreased precipitously from over two years 2,200 to 655 in 1788, because of ransoms paid and deaths. (Three of the seventeen American captives had died of disease by 1790.)

The American situation became even more perilous on Feb. 1, 1793, when post-revolutionary France declared war on England, Spain and Holland. This was a gale that roiled the seas of the world for decades. Later that year Portugal, with encouragement from England, made peace with Algiers. And within weeks Algerian ships were back on the offensive in the Atlantic. Quickly they seized 11 ships and more than 100 crewmen.

Jefferson's pleas for a response of naval strength to piracy now was echoed through the government. But Jefferson's own position was to take a strange turn. News of the new seizures in the Atlantic provoked an outcry from the public and the press. Mediterranean trade had been shut down by earlier Barbary attacks. Now Atlantic trade, even more essential to U.S. well-being, was under severe threat.

Insurance rates tripled on U.S. shipping in the Atlantic. And Americans were reminded frequently of their fellows enslaved in Algiers.

The idea of naval legislation, which had long been stalled in Congress, suddenly began to move quickly. The opposing sides in the political battle over the Navy resembled the forces that were forming the first political parties --- Federalists and Republicans. The Federalists were led by Jefferson's foe in Washington's administration, Treasury Secretary Alexander Hamilton.

Republicans (more Southern and agrarian) tended to be "anti-navalists". (This was the party that would elect Jefferson as President in 1800). Their opposition to the Navy was based on the belief that the existence of a Navy would attract foreign conflict and increase the public debt.

In March, 1794, "An Act to Provide Naval Armament" was passed by the Third Congress on a narrow vote and signed into law later that month by President Washington. It specified many operational details for a naval force such as pay (Captains would receive $75 per month and gunners $14 per month), and rations ("…Saturday, one pound of bread, one pound of pork, half a pint of peas or beans and four ounces of cheese…"). But more importantly it launched a successful technological strategy, authorizing the purchase or construction of four frigates with 44 guns each, and two with 36 guns. The 44 gun ships carried 8 more guns that other frigates, enabling them to win battles with some likely rivals. But a frigate's speed allowed these American vessels to outrun larger European ships.

There was a catch to the "Act to Provide Naval Armament" though. It required stopping construction of the six ships if peace could be dealt with Algiers and American prisoners freed.

The law creating the Navy appropriated $688,888.92 to build the six ships. Decisions on how to build the ships for that amount of money fell to Secretary of War Henry Knox. Fortunately, Knox quickly learned of two highly skilled maritime designers: Joshua Humphreys and Josiah Fox. He issued to them the commission for design of the six ships and they became America's first naval ship architects, and among its most distinguished.

Their innovative ideas gave the United States a technological edge in the Barbary conflict and later against much more sophisticated foes, like the Royal Navy in the War of 1812. Ironically, both Humphreys and Fox were Quakers.

The 44 gun American frigates were made possible by Humphrey's and Fox's design, which built a stronger vessel that was still capable of great speed. The early 19th century frigate fit in size between much larger (74 gun) line of battle ships, and much smaller and less heavily armed sloops and schooners. But the frigates designed by Humphrey and Fox carried firepower approaching a line battleship but were still capable of the speed of an earlier, lighter frigate.

Humphrey and Fox's design accomplished this through the use of intersecting diagonal "riders" that reinforced the ship's hull. These stanchions redistributed and spread the weight of the gundeck. At the same time, a new type of weapon was coming into use --- the carronade. This lighter gun could be positioned higher on the ship (where greater visibility assured greater accuracy) without jeopardizing a ship's seaworthiness. The combination of a stronger ship with powerful weaponry created American super-frigates, ships with the lethal force of battleships of the line, which also had the speed and elusiveness of a frigate.

As important as the innovative design, however, was a new material. The frames of the new ships would be built of strong and durable live oak, a material that grows only in the coastal Southeast of the United States. The distance of the material's habitat from the shipyards delayed construction and increased its cost, but it led to the finest frigates in the world.

Just as the arguments in the debate over the benefits of a strengthened defense force would sound familiar to 21st century Americans, the politics of the contracts for these ships would as well. These were attractive projects to shipbuilders so Washington and the Congress spread them among six port cities: Boston, New York, Philadelphia, Norfolk, Portsmouth and Baltimore. .

In the meantime, negotiations proceeded in Algiers. They were now under the direction of Colonel David Humphreys, an aide of Washington's going back as far as the Battle of Yorktown.

The demands made on the U.S. through its negotiators were particularly outrageous: some $1,080,000 paid to the Algerian treasury, plus private "emoluments" to the Dey of $540,000 and more than $600,000 in payoffs to a variety of the Dey's relatives, chamberlains, cooks and other members of his retinue.

Negotiations ended in September, 1795, with a treaty that was lauded by some at the time, but later viewed as disgraceful by many historians. In it the U.S. agreed to pay a ransom of $642,500, and annual tribute of $21,600 payable in naval stores including gunpowder, iron and bullets.

The Senate ratified the treaty on March 7, 1796. However, Humphreys and Barlow had difficulty borrowing the ransom money in war-torn Europe, so the American prisoners remained captive in Algiers and the Dey decided to keep negotiating.

To placate the Dey, Barlow (by now US diplomatic agent in Algiers) promised an additional gift of a 36 gun frigate, supposedly for the Dey's daughter. This commitment of Naval stores and promise of a ship were evidence of the inexperience or gullibility of the American negotiators (and of the Senate, which confirmed the resulting treaty). Naval and diplomatic historians have acknowledged the need to ransom the long-abused captives since no good alternative existed. But to make payment to such an incorrigible foe in the form of superior arms was both unprincipled and unwise.

Barlow eventually found a source for the cash ransom and paid it. On July 13, 1796 eighty-five freed American prisoners boarded a ship in Algiers bound for France ---thirty seven captives had died in Algerian slave quarters as a result of their imprisonment.

Work then stopped on the Navy shipbuilding in accord with the authorizing law. But Washington was now certain of the need for a naval force. Added to the Barbary threat, the conflict between England and France raged on the seas jeopardizing unprotected neutral shipping like that of the United States..

Washington sensed that the United States was in a position of real vulnerability as a mercantile and maritime nation. "The most sincere neutrality is not a sufficient guard against the deprivations of nations at war," he told Congress on Dec. 7, 1796. "To secure respect to a neutral flag requires a naval force, organized and ready to vindicate it from insult or aggression. This may even prevent the necessity of going to war...."

By that time he had already pushed Congress toward maintaining naval forces. His letter of March 15 had resulted in Congressional action in April authorizing the completion of three of the frigates with money remaining from the initial appropriation. Washington's terms as President were drawing to a close.

In the election of 1796 Adams was selected to succeed Washington. Besides having served as Washington's Vice-President, Adams had the experience of negotiating directly with Barbary states in London 10 years before. Earlier he led a committee of the Continental Congress that formed the American revolutionaries' naval force. With that experience, it is not surprising that Adams' support of building a naval force was strong and immediate.

Adams' old negotiating counselor Jefferson has been enticed into a very passive candidacy for President in 1796 also. Jefferson was sought out by his old Virginia friend James Madison to represent the fledgling Republican party. He had spent the three years since his retirement as Secretary of State in the peaceful pursuits of a farmer at Monticello. "I cherish tranquility too much to suffer political things to enter my mind at all," he wrote Washington.

Adams won the election and Jefferson came in second, making him Vice-President, under the rules of the era. Jeffersons's formal role involved presiding over the Senate. He also was the de facto head of the new Republican party. Through the emotional ties of that party and his early experience in Paris he had ties to France, just as the Federalists adopted a more conciliatory stance toward England.

Adams continued Washington's push for a naval force. In a speech to Congress in May, 1797, Adams called American commerce "an interesting object of attention," which if disrupted would cause "the most embarrassing disorders". He termed naval power "the natural defence of the United States", after an army or "militia".

He returned to address Congress in December, 1798, praising the "beneficial effects" of the small naval force in place, and urging "without loss of time" laying "the foundation for an increase of our Navy." 16

Peace reigned with the Barbary states based on treaties with Tripoli in 1796 and with Tunis in 1797. These were far less expensive than the price exacted by the Dey of Algiers. But Adams was alarmed about post-revolution France, which felt betrayed by American accommodation of England, its former colonial master and France's enemy. France broke off relations with the U.S. and encouraged its privateers to attack and seize American merchant shipping.

The War Department dithered in construction of the frigates and Adams moved decisively to speed things up. The Navy was created as a separate department of the government on April 30, 1798. Adams quickly appointed Benjamin Stoddert as the first Secretary of the Navy. Congress also authorized building or hiring of 12 smaller ships to supplement the six frigates already under construction.

The strength of the new frigate design and its speed was demonstrated in 1799 as the infant American Navy battled the French throughout the West Indies. The Constellation, commanded by Commodore Thomas Truxtun, captured the French frigate Insurgente off of Nevis. It also defeated the Vengeance in a five hour exchange of broadsides Southwest of Guadalope.

Several new ships came as gifts from American port cities. Stirred by the threats from France and from the corsairs, citizens lent labor and materials to construct four frigates. The smallest of them, the 32 gun Essex, was built in 1799 in Salem (Essex County), Massachusetts. It distinguished itself in later Barbary combat and became the first U.S. naval vessel to round both Cape Horn and the Cape of Good Hope. Similar efforts produced the Philadelphia and New York from those cities and the John Adams, built in Charleston, South Carolina

The war with France was closed by treaty just as Adams neared the end of his term as President. The Navy had been quite successful in defending growing American commerce and shipping from France's privateers and its Navy.

In 1800, Vice-president Jefferson won a close election for President over the incumbent Adams. The politics of their first contest had been subdued. This campaign was one of vilification by proxy, with Republican propagandists reviling Adams (calling him a warmonger among other things). Federalists responding with equal venom accusing Jefferson of an affection for France that bordered on treason, given the hostilities that existed between the two countries during the campaign.

Jefferson shortly would be faced with squaring his former aggressive Barbary negotiating posture with the anti-Navy views of his party. But before giving up the Presidency, Adams would send naval vessels carrying a diplomatic mission to the Mediterranean. The principal players and the strange twists of events previewed the hostilities that America would be engaged in for the first five years of the new century and of Jefferson's presidency.

Chapter IV

Thomas Jefferson was inaugurated on March 4, 1801, to head a nation that was on the edge of insolvency in a world of increasing hostilities. The new Republican party which he now headed was intent on shrinking the fledgling American military and was discussing disbanding its embryonic naval force. The nation was deeply in debt and lacked any ready method for repayment.

Jefferson's first inaugural address was a noteworthy attempt to unite a divided Congress and nation. This followed a particularly bitter and close election. The president recognized the need for some military security. But he directed more attention to the hostility emanating from Europe than the threat of piracy in the Mediterranean:

"During the throes and convulsions of the ancient world, during the agonizing spasms of infuriated man, seeking through blood and slaughter his long lost liberty, it was not wonderful that the agitation of the giant billows should reach even this distant and peaceful shore; that this should be more felt and feared by some and less by others, and should divide opinions as to measures of safety."

But reports from North Africa were ominous. The United States had sent a fledgling consular corps to the area in the hope of fostering peace and trade. Two members of this group were freed Barbary captives. James Leander Cathcart, who had managed to become Secretary to the Dey of Algiers for his captivity there, was sent to Tripoli, and Richard O'Brien, who had been Captain of the Dauphin when it was captured, was posted to Algiers, the city where he had been imprisoned.

The Tunis consul was William Eaton, a remarkable veteran of the Revolutionary War. Eaton would become a large actor in the conflict with the Barbary pirates, and his military role would make for one of the great adventures in American history, memorialized by poets and in the opening phrase of the Marine Corps Hymn. But Eaton's military role followed years in this diplomatic assignment plus naval cruises, embargoes and bombardments.

Cathcart quickly found that Barbary leaders used differences in tribute payments from Western nations to their advantage. They compared their own payments to those received by their brother pirate states. And each Barbary leader also seemed to have a good sense of what any given nation was paying their counterparts. This happened almost immediately in Tripoli, where the Bashaw informed Cathcart in April, 1799, that he had been promised a ship by U.S. diplomats (likely having heard of the frigate promised to the Dey of Algiers). "After an hour's bravado and huckstering," Cathcart reported, the Bashaw made his "ultimate" demand "the brig delivered to him immediately or the sum of eighteen thousand dollars on the spot in her lieu."

Cathcart's two colleagues were subjected to similar extortionate demands. Eaton reported having a consular gift to a Tunisian corsair admiral returned. In its place he demanded "a gold-headed cane, gold watch and chain and 12 pieces of cloth," Eaton noted. He reported to a colleague in Portugal that the Tunisians viewed the Americans as "a feeble sect of Christians and their independence was the gift of France".

And the Algerines, who had actually seized American ships, were not to be outdone. Their Dey expressed his wish to O'Brien for tamarinds and sweet meats, 20 dozen Madras handkerchiefs, 20 pieces of of Indian silk and large amounts of Irish linen, pimentos and pickled salmon.

All of this provoked O'Brien to register his early and strong argument for a Navy, citing "the great and urgent necessity of keeping up a Marine force, the frigates, sloops of war, brigs and schooners", and comparing the US consulates in North Africa to "lighthouses" warning American merchant vessels from "dangerous shoals".

In July, Eaton joined in, writing in the grandiose style that graced his diplomatic reports, that the "national interest, honour (and) safety demand a show of naval force in the Mediterranean."

The first US naval vessel set sail the next year, but with decidedly mixed results. The George Washington was a 24 gun frigate, which had been converted from its intended purpose as a merchant ship. It was commanded by William Bainbridge, only 26 years old at the time but already a veteran of the "quasi-war" with France. Bainbridge was dispatched to Algiers with tribute for the Dey, including "plank, some cables and a few canon, & some valuable European goods...", according to his orders.

But the U.S. Government also expected Bainbridge to project strength in Mediterranean harbors, perhaps the fledgling nation's first attempt at gunboat diplomacy. His orders read, "While you lay before (Algiers) keep up the strictest discipline, & the most Warlike appearance to make the best impressions of our discipline & power." In following this direction, Bainbridge suffered one truly embarrassing failure and one notable success.

The George Washington arrived in Algiers in September, 1800. Bainbridge, under the direction of a local harbor pilot, anchored under the Algerian fort that commanded the harbor. A few days later the Dey demanded the services of the George Washington, to carry slaves and other tribute to the Grand Porte in Constantinople. Bainbridge had unwittingly placed the ship in a vulnerable position and saw no good alternative but to comply. He later reported to Secretary of the Navy Benjamin Stoddert that refusing the request would have caused war, and slavery for the ship's 130-man crew. He described the Dey's attitude as "…you pay me tribute, by that you become my slaves, and then I have a right to order as I please."

So the next month the George Washington set sail for the capital of the Ottoman Empire bearing the Algerian Ambassador and a remarkable cargo of humans and goods: "20 gentlemen, 100 Negro Turks, 60 Turkish women, 2 lions, 2 tygers, 400 horses, 200 sheep…" plus jewels and money.+ How everyone fit on a 108 foot ship with a 130 man crew is a mystery to this day. The Algerine flag flew from the top of the mast (as ordered) when they got underway, but Bainbridge lowered it to a position below the U.S. flag once they had cleared port.

Nothing was comfortable in the 19-day voyage, including Muslim prayer. Five daily prayer sessions for the passengers were complicated by the ship's frequent tacking. To face Mecca, the worshipers needed to reorient themselves with each change of ship's heading. Eventually one man was posted to watch the compass and alert those praying to a shift in direction.

Bainbridge did significantly better in his second port call than in the first. He sailed quietly into the Ottoman harbor on November 9, 1800. In the morning, the Captain of the port saw the U.S. flag for the first time and questioned its origin. Bainbridge responded: "American frigate and colors", and later reported, "…they knew of no such place as America…".

The US flag won favor in Constantinople as it bore stars like the Ottoman flag. This heavenly object made an attractive contrast for the

Turks to the crests and shields of Europe. And Bainbridge was received as an exotic and honored guest.

He charmed the Sultan and his brother-in-law, the Naval Commander Capudan Pasha. As a mark of friendship on the George Washington's departure, Pasha gave Bainbridge a "firman", or passport, which ensured for safe passages throughout the Mediterranean.

Bainbridge had been aided in building good relationships with the Ottoman Admiral by two friendly faces: Lord Elgin, the British Ambassador; and Zacbe, the private secretary to the Pasha. Lord Elgin's intercession with the Turks on Bainbridge's behalf stood in marked contrast to the British diplomatic conniving that Americans had experienced earlier in Algiers. Not only was Lord Elgin a different man, but times had changed as the American Navy had battled in the Atlantic with England's great enemy, Napoleonic France.

Zacbe spoke fluent English and had some knowledge of the U.S. from diplomatic service in Paris where he had met Benjamin Franklin. Bainbridge formed a friendship with Zacbe that continued by letter long after the George Washington sailed from Istanbul.

The "firman" proved valuable when Bainbridge arrived back in Algiers in January, 1801 and he and Consul O'Brien went to call on the Dey. Amidst raucous threats and more intimidation, the Dey issued new orders for the George Washington and Bainbridge.

Bainbridge presented the firman. The Dey examined it and abruptly became deferential. Bainbridge then negotiated some concessions from the mollified Dey, including the release of 56 French captives. The George Washington carried them to freedom in Alicante, Spain.

The George Washington then returned to the U.S., arriving April 19, 1801, six weeks after Thomas Jefferson was inaugurated as the third President of the United States. The ongoing threats and hostilities in the Mediterranean were causing Jefferson to assemble a squadron to head there. Bainbridge's frustrating foray into hostile waters was rewarded with command of a more tradition man-of-war, the 32-gun frigate Essex.

Dispatching the squadron was a compromise between Jefferson's 1800 drive to shrink the Navy and reduce government debt, and the need to respond to new reports of threats to American vessels and citizens.

President Jefferson inherited a sizeable debt, a mandate to reduce government expenditures, and a law specifically authorizing a dramatic reduction in the size of the Navy. Had there been a federal budget during the Adams administration, it would have averaged about $11 million per year. Of that more than 40% went for debt service. The Navy, with annual expenditures of $2.5, million was a top target for Albert Gallatin, Jefferson's parsimonious and powerful Treasury Secretary.

Jefferson's administration pared the fleet back to 13 ships. Seven of the 13 were then deactivated in an additional measure to save money. One famous former naval officer, author and historian James Fennimore Cooper, regretted the cuts but found the selections of what to retain "effective".

Leadership was another issue. Jefferson's campaign to cut back the fleet made the post of Secretary of the Navy the slowest to be filled among his department heads. At one point Jefferson ruefully suggested he might advertise for someone to fill the post. Robert Smith, a Baltimore merchant who had supported Jefferson's political campaign, became interim Secretary of the Navy. Smith offered the squadron Commodore post to Thomas Truxtun, who had commanded a privateer in the Revolutionary War and skippered the new frigate Constellation in the quasi-war with France. Truxtun declined. He was critical of the restrictive description of the squadron's mission authorized by Congress, which he termed the "peace establishment"

On April 28 Smith selected Richard Dale to command the squadron. Barely two weeks later, and unaware of developments across the Atlantic, the Bashaw fulfilled his threat to declare war, using the traditional method of the region by chopping down the US flagpole in front of the consular mission "six feet from the ground" and leaving it "reclining on the terrace...", according to a letter from Cathcart.

Jefferson and his cabinet had broader goals for the squadron than making the Mediterranean safe for American merchant ships. The mission was also to focus heavily on training. The "great object", Smith advised, was to "direct our Young Officers in nautical knowledge generally, but particularly in the Shores & Coasts where you cruise."

He added that the President wanted "exact discipline" on board US Navy ships and the government soon issued Navy regulations for the commander of a squadron, signed by Secretary of the Navy Smith. These ranged from a broad directive like Number 9 (observed to this day), "He may suspend their employs the captains of vessels or any other officers under his command, who, by their bad conduct or other motives, he shall think deserving of such punishment...", to the ridiculously specific, "He is not to make use of ships sails for covering boats or for awnings."

Commodore Richard Dale had served ably in the Revolutionary Way as John Paul Jones' First Lieutenant. He was captured in that conflict, but escaped from a prisoner of war camp in a British officer's uniform.

Dale's squadron of four ships led by his flagship, the frigate President (44 guns) set sail on June 2, 1801. He was accompanied by two other frigates, Philadelphia (38) and Essex (32), plus a sloop-of-war Enterprise (12 guns) which was commanded by now relatively seasoned Bainbridge. The Philadelphia and Essex were "subscription ships", constructed with private funds in port cities that would benefit from a safe maritime and trade. (The Essex had been built in Essex County, Massachusetts by its residents.) A congressional act of June 30, 1798, had authorized the Navy to accept such ships built by citizens' subscriptions.

Dale's tactical orders from Smith were vague and somewhat contradictory (based on the direction that had been issued by Congress). This portended badly for the mission. The orders directed Dale head quickly to Gibraltar and determine if the U.S. was at war with any of the Barbary states. (Word of the Tripoli flagpole dismemberment had still not made it back to Washington.) He should then proceed from Gibraltar to Algiers and then on to Tunis where he was to deliver dispatches to US Consul William Eaton.

Finally Dale was directed to blockade Tripoli if he found the US at war with the Bashaw. At the same time, Smith issued unusual orders for clashes, "We enjoin on you the most rigorous moderation, conformity to right & reason and the suppression of all passions..." Jefferson in the meantime had written the Bashaw calling Dale's ships "a squadron of observation" and advising the Bashaw that the US wished to"...give umbrage to no power...."

This peacetime footing didn't last long, but the limitations on Dale's squadron affected it through its stay in the Mediterranean.

The squadron's Atlantic crossing was hampered by bad early summer weather. The smaller Enterprise was least affected in speed. Her commanding officer, Lt. Andrew Sterrett, was permitted to sail ahead alone and reached Gibraltar on June 29. There the ship's crew found they were anchored next to a Tripolitan schooner, the Meshuda, which in fact was the Betsey --- a Massachusetts ship seized by Tripolitan pirates five years before and renamed.

She was commanded by "Admiral Murad Reis" who in a previous life had been Peter Lisle, a Scottish deckhand on the Betsey when she was captured. Lisle had converted to the Muslim faith and eventually married the Bashaw's daughter (a sure path from deckhand to Admiral).

Dale and the remainder of his squadron reached Gibraltar three days later and the President anchored near the Enterprise, the Meshuda and the brig that accompanied Meshuda.

Dale asked Murad Reis if a state of war existed between the U.S. and Tripoli and Reis responded in the negative. But elsewhere throughout Gibraltar the Americans heard the opposite. They believed that the Tripolitan ships in Gibraltar had been headed to the Atlantic in order to attack American ships.

Dale detailed the Philadelphia, under the command of Capt. Samuel Barron, to guard Meshuda and her companion ship while Dale headed East into the Mediterranean with the rest of the squadron. The American squadron made stops in Tunis and Algiers en route to Tripoli. The Essex was assigned to the task of convoying merchants ships safely across the Mediterranean for the Atlantic, and the President and Enterprise headed to blockade Tripoli.

After a week on station there, Enterprise was ordered to Malta to restock both ships' water supplies. En route to Malta she ran into the Tripoli, a similarly gunned Tripolitan vessel commanded by Admiral Rais Mahomet Rous, and the first battle of the war ensued.

The Enterprise came upon Rous' ship Tripoli and hailed her. At first Sterrett's ship flew British colors (such deceptions were common place in sea battles in the early 19th century). Upon being hailed, the Tripoli came close by and Rous advised that his mission was in search for U.S. ships. Whereupon Sterrett shifted the Enterprise to her true colors and fired a broadside.

The American Captains had access to intelligence on the Barbary style of naval warfare. It involved coming alongside and using boarding parties armed with sabers and pistols.

"Their mode of attack is uniformly boarding," Eaton had reported about the Barbary corsairs (writing from Tunis in 1799). "Their long lateen yards drop on board the enemy and afford a safe and easy conveyance for the men who man them for this purpose." He continued, "...They throw (men) in from all points of rigging and from all quarters of the decks, having their sabers grasped in their teeth and their loaded pistols in their belts, that they have the full use of their hands in scaling the gunnels or netting of their enemy."

Rous followed form, attempting to board several times. But Sterrett's Enterprise was able to cast off and bombard the Tripoli repeatedly at shore range. The Tripoli feigned surrender twice only to resume fighting as soon as Enterprise loosened her grip. Finally, the third surrender was for real.

A boarding party from Enterprise found "the carnage on board was dreadful". The Tripoli had 30 men killed and 30 wounded of a total crew of 80.

Remarkably the Enterprise suffered no casualties. Enterprise's crew completed this engagement by dismasting the Tripoli and throwing her guns overboard. Then she was allowed to drift toward Tripoli, propelled by one small jury-rigged sail. There Rous was scorned by all including the Bashaw, who ordered him marched through the streets on a donkey before being subjected to 500 bastinadoes.

Sterrett's encounter with the Tripoli was the military high point of the Dale squadron's mission to be sure. A month later Dale abandoned the blockade, short of water and provisions and with many men on the doctor's list. Dale returned to Gibraltar on Sept. 25, 1801.

Dale found that the Meshuda and its accompanying brig had been abandoned in Gibraltar. Murad Reis and the ships' crews had apparently made their way back to Tripoli by other means. As such, there was no reason for Philadelphia to stand guard. Dale dispatched her to check in on Tripoli and then move on to Syracuse for the winter. The Essex would remain near Gibraltar. The Secretary of the Navy had ordered the President and Enterprise home.

Dale's problems continued when a harbor pilot ran President aground off of Port McMahon on the Mediterranean island of Minorca. The President then retired to the French port of Toulon for repairs.

Dale's Mediterranean cruise caused a strategy review by both the Navy and the Jefferson administration. Most significantly, Jefferson used his first address to Congress to raise the issue of the restrictive and vague orders under which Dale had sailed.

The Dec. 8, 1801 message to Congress recounted action to date in the war and particularly the Enterprise's battle:

"Our commerce in the Mediterranean was blockaded, and that of the Atlantic in peril. The arrival of our squadron dispelled the danger. One of the Tripolitan cruisers having fallen in with, and engaged small schooner Enterprise, commanded by Lieutenant Sterret, which had gone as a tender to our larger vessels, was captured, after a heavy slaughter of her men, with the loss of a single one on our part. The bravery exhibited by our citizens on that element, will, I trust, be a testimony to the world that it is not the want of that virtue which makes us seek their peace...."

Then the President recounted Sterrett's release of the disabled Tripoli in conformance with their orders and posed the issue of the adequacy of those orders to Congress:

" The legislature will doubtless consider whether, by authorizing measures of offence, also, they will place our force on an equal footing with that of its adversaries. I communicate all material information on this subject, that in the exercise of the important function confided by the constitution the legislature exclusively, their judgment may form itself on a knowledge and consideration of every circumstance of weight."

Congress responded two month later with orders that allowed the Navy to commit more fully to battle in its "Act for the Protection of the Seamen of the United States, against the Tripolitan Cruisers." It directed the Navy to "...subdue, seize and make prizes of all vessels, goods and effects, belonging to the Bey of Tripoli..."

Dale's task force had tested some of the main naval strategies of the war including blockades, convoys and logistics over a broad geography of varying hostility. He advised the need for a larger force, and particularly pushed the need for gunboats in future squadrons. The gunboats' shallower drafts would allow them to maneuver safely far nearer the shore of this reef and shoal laden, and largely uncharted coast.

Congress' tougher orders and the Navy's more informed strategy would come into play with the Navy in the Mediterranean. But that would be only after the 1802 "Morris squadron", one of the notable embarrassments in the early history of the American Navy.

Chapter V

The search for Dale's successor covered old ground. Captain Thomas Truxtun was offered command of the Chesapeake and the squadron by the new Secretary of the Navy Robert Smith (brother of the interim Secretary Samuel Smith). Truxtun demanded a Captain under him to command the Chesapeake while he directed the squadron from the ship's bridge. When Smith declined, Truxtun threatened to refuse the command for the second time (having turned it down prior to Dale's mission) and resign his commission.

With Jefferson and Congress cutting the size of the Navy drastically, Smith denied Truxtun's demand and accepted his resignation.

Smith's next move was not as wise. He selected Richard Morris, from a prominent political family to assume the Mediterranean command. Richard Morris was the son of Lewis Morris, a signer of the Declaration of Independence, and nephew of Gouvernor Morris, a member of the Constitutional Convention. Also, interestingly, in the 1800 Presidential election Richard Morris' brother Lewis Robert Morris helped swing a tied

Congressional vote to Jefferson on the 36th ballot through the abstention of the Vermont delegation along with Maryland, Delaware and South Carolina. This won Jefferson the Presidency over Aaron Burr.

The political connection has been noted by historians, but there appears to be no known direct tie to Richard Morris' ill-fated Navy appointment.

The next step in Morris' appointment presaged the relaxed and tragic-comic nature of his squadron's 1803 deployment. Morris' wife petitioned Smith for permission to accompany her husband. Smith responded to Morris on April 2, 1802 advising Morris that he had granted this request from "your lady" that she, her young son and his nursemaid be allowed to sail with the Chesapeake.

Mrs. Morris was among several females accompanying the flagship's officers and crew. Throughout the voyage the women's lives (and the lives of their offspring) wove through the ship's life as a colorful source of stories and gossip. Later, Midshipman Henry Wadsworth's journal acidly noted Mrs. Morris' knowledge of history and geography and added: "… her person is not beautiful or even handsome, but she looks very well in a veil…." The journal even included a (caricature) coat of arms for the Morris family: "Commodore seated on a match tub, his lady in a chair by his side, Gerard (their infant son) between them each having a hand on each side of a nine-pounder mounted with the implements of War: at their backs on the bulwark are fixed battle axes in the form of a half moon & a row of shot in a shot locker."

Wadsworth later recounted the on-board baptism of the infant son of a Chesapeake crew member and his lady attended by five of her peers, but others who apparently were not invited to the ceremony and "got drunk in their quarters out of pure spite." (Wadsworth's family would distinguish itself in letters. He was the uncle of great American poet Henry Wadsworth Longfellow.)

The Chesapeake was beaten to Gibraltar by Constellation, commanded by Capt. Alexander Murray. The Chesapeake had sprung her mainmast in storms during the crossing and retired to the British yards for repairs upon arrival. Murray's ship was dispatched to Tripoli to begin a blockade. He found an ally there in Sweden, which had also lost its flagpole in Tripoli and was trying to enforce a blockade of the port.

In July, off of Tripoli the Constellation engaged a group of eight Barbary gunboats commanded by Murad Reis. (Reis had abandoned his ships in Gibraltar and had found other transport back.) Constellation chased the gunboats toward port. Murray was stopped by shoal waters too shallow for the frigates, and had to be satisfied with firing futilely at the boats and shore from ½ mile range. The encounter drew the Tripolitan army, which stormed around the beach to little effect.

The encounter revealed a flaw in American strategy for the makeup of its fleet. While the frigates were fast and well armed, the American Navy lacked small ocean going vessels that could operate reliably close to shore. This weakness was to reveal itself tragically and dramatically further on in the war.

The ineffectiveness of the Murray blockade was also clear in the fate of the Philadelphia merchant brig Franklin, its Captain Andrew Morris and its crew who were captured off of Cape Palos, Spain. While the captive vessel and her cargo were dispatched to the West Indies, the crew was carried to Tripoli in their captors' vessels undeterred by the American squadron.

More frustrating still was the seeming indifference of the Constellation and the Swedish ship off of Tripoli, which received a salute from the corsair vessel bearing the captives and then allowed it to sail on and into Tripoli. The two ships, Andrew Morris wrote Cathcart, "never made the least effort to obstruct our progress when it was certainly in their power to Capture or run the Pirate on shore." The merchant skipper also suggested a more coherent strategy than Morris attempted: "...one or two fast sailing vessels and a frigate stationed off Cape Bon would effectually intercept every thing belonging to the enemy going through between the Barbary shore, and the Island of Sicily..."

By September, the crew of the Franklin had been freed by negotiation. Several sailors claimed British or French citizenry and were freed and five Americans, including the Captain, were ransomed for $1,000 each paid to the Bashaw.

The Swedish vessels left the blockade to get supplies, leaving the Constellation to carry out an even more feckless blockade on its own. This performance coupled with the complete absence of the Commodore and his flagship from the area of conflict stirred Consul William Eaton.

Eaton succumbed easily and quickly to bombast and the Morris squadron was a tempting target for it. Eaton compared the Chesapeake's voyage bearing the Commodore and Mrs. Morris to the adventure of Anthony and Cleopatra, adding the suggestion that in lieu of a blockade the U.S. government should "station a company of comedians and a seraglio before the enemy's port", and took to referring to Murray in his correspondence as "Old Woman Murray".

Eaton's conflict with Murray had erupted soon after the Constellation reached Gibraltar. Traditionally military leaders and some European diplomats had mixed private enterprise and government service (the naval practice of taking prizes and dividing the spoils of such captures being best known.)

Eaton mixed his own business with that of the U.S. in the Mediterranean (often to the benefit of the U.S. as well as himself). When Morris' and Murray's ships had arrived in the Mediterranean Eaton had a vessel, the Gloria, that was also under orders to attack Tripolitan shipping. Murray had encountered Gloria early on in Gibraltar and had withdrawn funding or supplies for the privateer.

There was a natural tension between the fairly novice naval officers and the completely inexperienced consular corps almost from the start. But the spectacle of Morris' flagship sailing decorously among the European ports of the Mediterranean while Tripoli lay largely unguarded brought open conflict.

Nearly every ship carrying mail from the squadron to the U.S. bore letters from Eaton and Cathcart complaining to Secretary of State James Madison about the diplomats' view of the naval squadron's ineffectiveness. Similar entreaties from Murray and Morris were sent beseeching Secretary of the Navy Robert Smith.

Eaton often started things. The "government may as well send out quaker meeting houses to float around this sea as frigates with Murrays in command," he wrote Madison in August, 1802.

This was somewhat unfair to Murray, as he was bereft of any communication or direction from his seniors, particularly the Commodore. He was attempting a blockade essentially unaided. In the months in the Mediterranean, Murray wrote Morris, he had been "in hourly expectation of some information or instructions from our government...."

Murray expressed dissatisfaction with the blockade he had been able to conduct. He noted the need for more ships, particularly small ones that could sail and flight close to shore.

Two days later Murray jumped rank, expressing his frustration in a letter to Secretary of the Navy Smith: "...I found here a few Lines from Capn. Morris who doth not say whether it is his intention or not to come up this way, neither does he furnish me with any instructions, so that I must guide myself by my own judgment and act as I deem most expedient." From that point Murray on his own began to report to Smith and seek his direction in lieu of any from Morris.

The argument for small ships, advanced forcefully by Dale, Murray and others finally took hold in Congress early the next year when an appropriation was passed to build four ships of up to 16 guns apiece for a total of $96,000, and 15 gunboats for $50,000.

While the Morris squadron had an ignominious reputation as a combatant force, it was known for its duels.

Two Marine officers from the Constellation dueled over a since forgotten slight while the ship was in Leghorn, Italy. There Lt. Richard H.L. Lawson shot Captain James McKnight through the heart at six paces. Murray had Lawson and his second arrested.

Later in Malta Midshipman Joseph Bainbridge (William's younger brother) was part of a group of Americans who were mocked and bumped repeatedly in the lobby of a Valetta hotel. Bainbridge scored a knockdown on a Mr. Cochran (the Secretary to Malta's

British Governor General). A challenge was then issued by the Englishman, an experienced dueler.

The inexperienced young Bainbridge had Stephen Decatur as a second and coach. Based on Decatur's counsel Bainbridge specified a duel distance of four paces instead of the customary ten. Cochran's reputation and confidence may have exceeded his skill, as at this short distance he missed completely. Bainbridge didn't, killing Cochran with his second shot after creasing his hat with his first.

The aggrieved British Governor sought to arrest Bainbridge and Decatur, but they were spirited out of Malta under suspension by the Navy. They were cleared by an investigation in Washington, and both returned to the Mediterranean with the Navy on a new Navy brig, Argus, in 1803.

As 1802 ended Morris had yet to take any blockading action off Tripoli himself --- not even a simple reconnoiter of the coastline from off shore. Murray and Constellation had returned home and other ships were being shifted or were undergoing repairs.

Morris made an attempt to reach Tripoli in January, 1803, but he was driven off by storms.

At that moment, Eaton sought his aid in Tunis with an oblique warning message: "Affairs of incalculable moment to the United States here require the assistance of your counsel, perhaps your force."

Morris arrived to find the Bey threatening war. This was principally over the fate of a Turkish ship, Paulina, which had been seized by the Enterprise. Tunis and Tripoli both had some stake in the Paulina's cargo. Unless recompense was made, Tunis threatened to join Tripoli at war with the U.S.

After a long argumentative meeting with the Bey, Morris agreed to a settlement on Paulina's cargo based on a generous comparison between the Bey's manifest and the Paulina's bill of lading. Several days later the Bey demanded more cargo not included on his bill of lading plus $34,000 he claimed had been pledged in payments by Eaton.

When Eaton resisted, he was called "mad" and ejected from Tunis, according to the account of Cathcart, who sat in on the meeting with Morris and Eaton. The Bey's ejection of Eaton came as no great surprise. Eaton had written Madison six months earlier, describing his position in Tunis as "insupportable." In that letter he wrote, "From the first moment of my agency here it was apparent to me that submission to the demands of this Bey would only sharpen avidity." He later added a postscript to the letter advising that he had just been summoned to the Palace where one of the Bey's ministers had just demanded the delivery of a 36-gun frigate as an additional gift.

So the American party finally offered the prospect of a new consul, cash and cargo to secure peace. It was a low point for Eaton who emerged from the meeting broke and without a job. Eaton's loss of his job was no blow to Morris, who had grown to detest him, doubtless in large part due to Eaton's correspondence to Washington.

The contretemps in Tunis ended when the squadron sailed for Algiers on March 13 with Rodgers and Cathcart joining Eaton. They headed to Algiers to pick up O'Brien, who was retiring, and then on to Gibraltar.

Eaton transferred to a merchant ship for transit back to the U.S. It would turn out to be quite appropriately named for a vessel bearing him ---"Perserverance". He was headed to Washington to revive his career and push a plan for Tripoli that he had quietly concocted during his time in Tunis.

In April, 1803, Morris marked the first anniversary of his Mediterranean command still not having sailed in the waters off of Tripoli for a single hour. The Chesapeake headed home and Morris moved his flag to the New York. The Constellation had completed its deployment earlier, heading back to the United States in March.

As weather improved in late April, Morris decided to attempt Tripoli from his post on board New York with Enterprise as an escort. They planned to meet the John Adams and Adams (two different Navy vessels) along the way.

En route past Sardinia an explosion in a gunner's storeroom devastated the New York. A lit candle left by a gunner's mate in a storeroom caused a horrible explosion and fire, killing 14 crewmembers and severely burning many more. Fortunately, the fire didn't reach the ship's main magazine or the ship would have been destroyed.

At the beginning of May, New York reached Malta badly in need of first aid and repairs, which took about three weeks to restock. While the New York was laid up in Malta with Enterprise, Rodgers headed for Tripoli on the John Adams. He showed his more aggressive stance almost immediately. On May 12, John Adams intercepted a ship trying to avoid the blockade. It turned out to be a familiar face with another new name: the flagship Meshuda (the captured Betsey) which Murad Reis had abandoned in Gibraltar when he realized exit from that port was blocked long term by the U.S. Navy. Meshuda bore papers issued by the Empire of Morocco, but the John Adams crew found she carried guns, cutlasses and other war supplies so Rodgers took her to Malta.

The Meshuda bore a passport issued by Consul James Simpson of Morocco. However, the passport specifically forbade trading with a power under American blockade. Finally on the morning of May 22 (almost one year after entering the Mediterranean) Morris cast his gaze on the Tripolitan coast. The ships John Adams and Enterprise accompanied New York and six days later Adams joined up with them.

A target appeared almost immediately in the form of a 25 ton felucca (a lateen rigged fast vessel, typically North African) which Enterprise chased until it was beached. Morris on New York drew close and a plan to tow the vessel off the beach with ships' boats was debated. Morris nixed the mission to the apparent dissatisfaction of some on board: "We were all very much disappointed at not being permitted to tow her off," Wadsworth observed. But whether the protective fire of the squadron would have been sufficient protection to withstand the Tripolitan army is doubtful.

On June 1, Enterprise reported a group of about 10 feluccas beached in a bay 35 miles to the West of the city. Their skippers claimed they carried grain, but they were unwilling to allow a search. They were guarded by cavalry brandishing swords and muskets.

An American reconnaissance party of two boats led by Lieutenants David Porter and James Lawrence and Midshipman Wadsworth approached the boats on a moonlit night. They overheard the crew as they approached, but were discovered fairly quickly. A brief gun battle ensued prior to the boats, officers and 10 crewmen returning to the Enterprise and New York.

The scouting mission was followed by a daylight expedition in greater force intended to capture the feluccas or destroy their cargo. Nine boats bore 50 men under Porter's command. The Tripolitans fired at the American party from a distance, save one Tripolitan who tried from closer range and was quickly killed. Five Americans were wounded in the gun battle. The feluccas were set afire, but to limited practical effect as the Tripolitans were able to extinguish the fires and salvage most of the cargo.

Morris then made an attempt at negotiation. Jefferson had set a two-handed strategy based on a show of military force, followed by a peace negotiated from what he hoped would be a position of strength. Apparently, Morris believed that a raid on a group of small cargo boats was a demonstration of power. After an exchange of messages and guarantees of safety, the two parties met. When the Commodore emerged from the final session he reported the Bashaw's demand of $200,000 and $20,000 plus unspecified (but doubtless escalating) military and Naval stores annually. Morris said no, and shortly after departed for Malta, leaving Enterprise, John Adams, and Adams to maintain a blockade. (Morris, who required little reason to schedule a port call, had more reason for this one. His wife had delivered a son during his venture to Tripoli.)

Rodgers was in command of the remaining force and soon made well of the opportunity. On the night of June 21, he noticed unusual activity in the harbor portending ship movements. Rodgers arranged his force to prevent anyone leaving or entering the port. Enterprise detected a 22-gun Tripolitan polacre attempting to enter the harbor. Rodgers on John Adams closed on the polacre and battered it in a 45-minute exchange of cannon fire.

The Tripolitan crew began to abandon ship but Rodgers had to veer off to avoid shoal water near the harbor. He prepared boats and boarding parties to complete the capture but that proved unnecessary. The polacre exploded spectacularly, shooting masts, sails and rigging 150 feet in the air by Rodgers' estimate.

There were no casualties in the American squadron. Losses among the estimated 200-man crew of the polacre were heavy. Morris summoned the remainder of the squadron back from the blockade, and they had all abandoned the effort by June 30.

Jefferson was livid with Morris' feeble efforts and doubtless perplexed by the communications from his Mediterranean consular corps to Madison. Morris could have taken warning from a May 4 letter from Secretary of the Navy Smith noting that he (like Murray) had received little to no communication from the Commodore: "I presume it would be superfluous to remind You of the absolute necessity of your writing frequently and keeping us informed of all your movements," Smith wrote. While such a reminder should have been "superfluous", apparently it was not.

While Morris was engaged in his sole mission to Tripoli, Jefferson and Smith were intent on replacing him with a Commodore appropriate to the orders they had issued with the approval of Congress. Fortunately, they would soon succeed.

Meanwhile Rodgers was designated to an interim status in command of the squadron. Morris received orders advising that he was "suspended" at the "command of the President" and ordered him back to the U.S. "without delay."

Chapter VI

With Tripoli's declaration of war and the clear weakness of the American squadron under Morris the American diplomats O' Brien and Cathcart received a series of intimidating gestures and outright threats from Morocco and Algiers. The consuls' positions had become quite untenable as they attempted to respond resolutely with little effective naval strength in support.. Eaton had been driven out of Tunis. O'Brien tried to leave Algiers but the Dey told him he would not accept Cathcart as a replacement. He said Cathcart was too hostile to Algiers' interest. The fledgling Mediterranean diplomatic corps was also compromised by their colleagues in Washington, who were slow in delivering tribute that had been promised to the three other Barbary states as the Tripolitan war continued.

America's heavy debt was a barrier to any show of naval strength. Jefferson and the Republicans had won election in 1800 pleading debt reduction, tax relief and economy in government. In the Adams years, about 40% of each federal budget had been consumed by debt service. Treasury Secretary Gallatin intended to solve that by rapidly paying down principal. He targeted savings in naval expenses as the biggest source of funds to pay down the debt.

Jefferson's position was schizophrenic and untenable. He was attempting to project strength, and at the same time cutback the only U.S. forces that embodied such strength. This was an ongoing battle throughout Jefferson's first term, with Gallatin advocating continuous and dramatic reductions in the fleet and Smith resisting cuts and at times proposing increases.

Jefferson had more pressing issues to deal with, particularly one huge opportunity. As the political battles continued and the war dragged on, the President was moving forward on a priceless investment, but one which would bring a big new requirement for funds. With France's diminished colonial opportunities in the Americas, Jefferson believed Napoleon could be induced to sell the Louisiana Territory. Such a purchase would elevate the United States' prospects and stature, but would complicate the effort to stabilize the government's weak financial situation.

The decision to relieve Morris was going on as Jefferson was executing his strategy to induce France to make a massive land sale. Meanwhile, Eaton had arrived in Washington urging a more aggressive war posture on the administration and Congress.

Gallatin continued to scratch for new ways to economize. Amidst these conflicting currents, Jefferson recast strategy for the Navy and its Mediterranean expedition.

When Jefferson took office there had been a clear need for him to focus on the national debt. The Adams administration was spending about 40% of its annual budget servicing the federal debt, which stood at $83 million when he handed the reins to Jefferson.

The debt dwarfed the government's annual revenues of $10,600,000 (mainly from customs duties). Gallatin's plan had attacked the main other area of government expenditure --- military spending. By doing so he increased the annual payments on the debt by 62% to $7,300,000. At that rate he projected the debt would be paid off in 16 years. The plan called for drastic reductions in the ongoing costs of government, particularly the Navy. Its budget in 1802 was down 63% from the average year of the Adams administration.

Jefferson's dilemma is made clear by communication between him and his cabinet during the period in which Morris foundered and the administration pondered his replacement. Despite the threat from Morocco, Jefferson considered the wisdom of withdrawing ships, noting the presence of the Chesapeake, the Adams and the Constitution "two of them are thought sufficient for the war (in) Tripoli, especially while Sweden cooperates. In the present state of things would it not be advisable to let the three remain or does it seem necessary to send another," he asked Madison in August, 1802. Old alternative strategies were debated again including tribute or an alliance with lesser European powers like Sweden. Jefferson directed "a liberal attention ... to the interests of Sweden in the Mediterranean anticipating "a permanent league of the powers of war" with the Barbary states.

Madison stood less firm than Jefferson on tribute. When Morocco declared war in 1802, Madison favored sending this hostile nation previously promised gun carriages noting "the anxiety and the ideas" of Gallatin. Fortunately Jefferson withheld arms from Morocco while it was showing hostility to the U.S. But he relented when the Emperor moderated. Jefferson pushed to expedite delivery of promised supplies to Algiers to hold off hostilities there due to unfulfilled promises. Jefferson called his tactic "a steady course of justice aided occasionally with liberality."

Jefferson's inventive mind also was attracted to naval strategy. The need for a more permanent naval force had become clearer during the Mediterranean war, and with tensions with France and England. But Jefferson lamented the risk of provocation and the necessary and recurring expense posed by such a force. So he investigated ways that ships could be safely stored and repaired between deployments.

In November, 1802, Jefferson engaged architect Benjamin Latrobe in planning a new type of dry dock. This would rely on water from streams flowing down steep hillsides near the naval yard to flood and drain the dry docks. The large planned docks (big enough for 12 frigates) would be sited above tide level, covered by roofs and filled by streams running down from 30 to 200 feet above the docks.

In a letter to Latrobe, Jefferson asked him to draw up plans and a budget for this engineering project. He noted that the European drydocks in contrast were "...all very expensive in their construction..."

While Congress never moved ahead to fund Jefferson's plan, it wasn't for lack of specifics: he had even pointed out three Washington area streams that could provide the plumbing for the project --- the Eastern Branch, Tyber and Rock Creek. (Latrobe did have a lasting effect on Washington architecture through a redesign and reconstruction of some sections of the U.S. Capitol building.)

William Eaton arrived in Washington and found Jefferson and his cabinet in heavy pursuit of the Louisiana Purchase, while they also worried about the country's heavy load of debt. They were attempting to stay safe and balanced in the war between two world powers: England and France.

Eaton bore two dramatic and grand proposals on reaching the capital. The first --- an American expeditionary force of 5,000 troops headed to North Africa --- received polite attention, but not serious consideration from Jefferson's cabinet or Congress.

Eaton introduced the idea while closeted with Jefferson and Madison on April 25 shortly after his arrival in Washington. Eaton recalled the President as "reserved" and stated that the Secretary of War viewed his troop plan as "too great an effort and expense".

Jefferson referred the Barbary matter to his cabinet, which heard Eaton present his proposal on May 11. Only one official, Secretary of the Navy Smith, offered support.

Eaton then retreated to his fallback, an audacious plan that he had been nurturing for more than two years. He proposed to recruit Hamet Karamanli, the Bashaw's younger brother, to dispose of his brother, Jusuf, the ruler of Tripoli, and then claim power.

The bloody history of the Karamanli family did provide fertile ground for insurrection. The Bashaw, Jusuf, had himself gained the path to his throne by murdering their oldest brother, Hassan, about the time the Karamanlis' father died. Later Jusuf, the youngest of the three brothers claimed the role of Bashaw after having frightening Hamet into fleeing he country. Hamet retreated to Tunis where he encountered Eaton, who was in his role as consul.

From that chance meeting in 1801 Eaton began to form a plan that he would propose to Jefferson in Washington two years later when the American expeditionary force was rejected. Could the US install Hamet, who could claim right to the title of Bashaw by precedence, in place of the Americans' enemy, Jusuf, who had gained power through murder?

Eaton found Hamet willing (in part based on some $22,000 that Eaton had advanced to him). Jusuf had been attempting to induce Hamet to move to the Tripolitan city of Derna by proffering a role as Governor. Eaton feared a trap and warned Hamet that he likely would share his brother Hassan's fate, if he fell under Jusuf's control.

When Eaton had first tried to secure support for his plan, he had already been rejected by Murray and Morris. However, when he protested in a letter to Secretary of State Madison, he had received vague support from a higher level of the government:

"Although it does not accord with the general sentiments or views of the United States, to intermeddle in the domestic contests of other countries, it cannot be unfair, in the prosecution of such a just war, or the accomplishment of a reasonable peace, to turn to their advantage, the enmity and pretensions of others against a common foe. How far success in the plan ought to be relied on cannot be decided at this distance, and with so imperfect a knowledge of many circumstances. The event, it is hoped, will correspond with your zeal and with your calculations."

But Eaton's plan needed military support more than Madison's words, and the naval commanders in the Mediterranean didn't offer any. During a brief foray to Derna on his own, Hamet had appealed for American help in regaining the throne.

In a letter to Jefferson written early in 1803 in which he related his claims upon the office from his brother, who he said was holding members of Hamet's family against their will, Hamet asserted

"Therefore I am determined to go there with an hundred thousand men and take him and them too." he wrote.

But with the Navy commanders offering no support, Hamet knew he was vulnerable. He secretly departed Derna for Egypt. He was in hiding there in 1803 when Eaton resurfaced the plan with Jefferson, in person this time. Eaton had been scheduled to meet with Madison and the President, but Madison was ill. So only Jefferson and Eaton were present. Eaton had been hard at work putting his new plan together to restore Hamet using a band of mercenaries he would recruit in the region. Jefferson's response to the plan was not recorded. However, Eaton received very practical support (the pledge of $40,000 in cash and 1,000 rifles) plus a new title (United States Naval Agent on the Barbary Coast).

The new title and Eaton's place in the organizational chart of the little U.S. government made matters quite unclear. His countrymen were left to wonder what his formal reporting relations were to both the State Department and the Navy. This foggy situation gave Eaton considerable latitude. He would use it dramatically and to full effect when he returned to the Mediterranean.

In the meantime, the Naval presence in the Mediterranean was about to be strengthened radically, both in ships and leadership. Jefferson appointed an experienced Navy Captain, Edward Preble, to lead the squadron. Preble, the son of an influential Maine landowner and colonial military leader, had been going to sea since he was 18. He had commanded the Essex on a solo mission to rescue American merchantmen in Java. As such, Essex was the first American Naval vessel to cross the Equator and round the Cape of Good Hope.

After the Essex's return, Preble's health declined causing him to have to pass up command of the Adams in the Morris squadron. (What would have happened with the strong and aggressive Preble serving under the desultory Morris is hard to imagine.)

When Morris was recalled, Preble's health had improved. (However, he suffered off and on for the rest of his life from what his biographer Christopher McKee has concluded was a case of ulcers.) In Smith's July, 1803, order directing Preble's leadership of the squadron, he granted great latitude, noting that the situation and distance "...render it improper for the government to prescribe to you any particular course of conduct." Smith did specify that Jefferson had an expectation of an "effectual blockade of Tripoli...."

Fortunately, that was all the direction that Preble needed to dramatically change the course of the war.

Chapter VII

Edward Preble sailed to assume his Mediterranean command out of Boston in August, 1803. He was the antithesis of the commodores who had confronted Tripoli to date in the conflict. He would become a model for scores of American Naval leaders who followed him.

It was quickly clear that the new Commodore was a dramatic change in leadership style. Preble's reputation was that of an officer with a ferocious temper and a stern demeanor. Not surprisingly, he used the Atlantic crossing to impose a purposeful organization and strict discipline on the Constitution's officers and crew.

This new war stance of the Constitution became clear on the night of September 10, when a lookout spied the silhouette of a vessel in the haze off of the Atlantic port of Cadiz, Spain. The ship was unresponsive when asked its identity. Threats were exchanged. The stranger finally announced itself as the British capital ship Donegal (84). It demanded Preble send over the Constitution's boat. "This is the United States Ship Constitution, 44 guns, an American Commodore, who will be damned before he sends his boat on board of any vessel!", Preble shouted in response.

After a few minutes of silence a boat approached the Constitution bearing a British officer who explained the ship was actually a British frigate, the Maidstone. It was clear from that point that Preble's hard demeanor was not just for show.

Before Preble could employ this new stance on the Bashaw, he had to employ it with the Sultan of Morocco. As Morris completed his Tripoli tour, the three other Barbary states were issuing new threats (perhaps from having observed the frivolous actions of the Morris squadron). But the first real hostilities came from the Moroccans.

William Bainbridge's Philadelphia had proceeded across the Atlantic before Preble. Coming along the Spanish coast en route to the straits of Gibraltar, Bainbridge captured the Moroccan cruiser Mirboka and its American merchant prize, the brig Celia out of Boston. After being captured by Bainbridge, the Mirboka's skipper Rais Lubarez produced his orders directing him to capture American merchant ships. He said they had been issued by Alcayde Abd Al-Rahman, the Governor of Tangiers. Bainbridge took the two vessels to Gibraltar to await Preble. In the meantime was able to get the content of Lubarez's orders confirmed independently.

James Simpson, US Consul to Morocco, confronted Governor Al-Rahman with this information in Tangiers. Al-Rahman quickly responded by denying that he had issued the orders. He then told Simpson he would be detained until the Moroccan ships were returned (including the previously captured Meshuda).

So when Preble arrived in Gibraltar a conflict with Morocco had begun. He gained control over two captured Moroccan cruisers plus an American merchant vessel that one of them had seized. He also learned that the US Consul to the Moroccan Emperor was under house arrest. Preble's response again defined the vast shift in leadership that had taken place with his appointment by Jefferson.

He wrote Simpson of Morocco's "late gross violation of our treaty" that justified an American order to "capture and bring into port all vessels belonging to the Emperor of Morocco....". If a Moroccan vessel captured another American ship, Preble wrote "… you may acquaint the Emperor from me, that it is my intention in future to skin every such vessel as a pirate...."

Preble ordered Philadelphia and Vixen, under Bainbridge's command, to Tripoli to reattempt a blockade. On Sept. 17, 1803, Preble on Constitution, with the ship John Adams accompanying, sailed for Tangiers with Lubarez and his fellow Moroccan officers accompanying Preble.

Upon their arrival, the Americans received messages from shore by boat. Hidden in the mailbag was a note from Simpson warning that the brig Hannah out of Salem, Massachusetts, had been captured by Moroccans in the Atlantic off of their trading port of Mogador.

The Sultan was in Meguines and wasn't due to return to Tangiers until early October. In the meantime, Preble tried out the principal American argument on Lubarez and his colleagues: Why fight when you can gain more by trading with us? The conversation went on through Manna, an interpreter Preble had brought from Gibraltar.

Lubarez was experienced, as he had served for two years as the Moroccan Ambassador to Spain, and Preble pronounced him a "sensible, considerate and well informed man." Preble's case was simple:

"That the emperor (would) be much more benefited by our Commerce, than he could by a war with us ---That our Commerce extended to all nations, which would enable us to carry to the Moors everything they could want; besides what was produced in our own Country; and that we should take from them such things as they had to dispose of, which (would) be very profitable to the Merchants, as well as productive to the Revenue of the Emperor --- That our Shipping was very numerous & powerful --- That we (would) strive all in our power to keep peace with them upon proper and honorable terms; but if we were obliged to go to war, we should not only destroy all their vessels, which (would) not require much of our force to do; but we should send ships and batter down every Sea Port Town in the Empire"

Preble remained near Tangiers awaiting word of the Emperor's return, which finally happened on Oct. 4. The Constitution and Preble arrived the next day accompanied by Lear, the captive Moroccan officers (the crew remained in Gibraltar on board Meshuda, which had been converted to a prison ship). The Emperor paraded 2,500 troops in a display of military muscle. Preble responded with 21 gun salutes from Constitution and her escorts New York and John Adams.

The Emperor's peaceable intentions then became quite clear when he had 10 bullocks and 20 sheep delivered to the American squadron. More importantly, he ordered the release of Hanna from Magador before meeting with the Americans.

After several days of severe gales, Preble finally met with the Emperor on Oct. 11, accompanied by Lear and two Midshipmen. One of the Midshipmen, Ralph Izard, found the Emperor a disappointing presence, "…a small man, wrapped up with a woolen haik or cloak sitting upon the steps of an old castle…." The Moroccan ruler blamed the seizure of American ships on Governor Alcayde, who he promised to punish "more than to our satisfaction," Izard reported.

All in all, the strengthened American squadron under Preble's aggressive leadership worked to full and fast effect. The new Emperor reconfirmed the treaty with the U.S., signed by his father, and extended it indefinitely. Both sides agreed to release ships and prisoners they had seized.

In an Oct. 11 letter to President Jefferson and the U.S. Senate, the Emperor offered assurances that all treaties between the U.S. and Morocco "remain as they were and they shall not be altered or changed". Preble forwarded the Moroccan's correspondence through

Madison, suggesting that Jefferson communicate annually to forestall the Emperor feeling slighted.

Preble's early success in meeting the first challenge of his leadership role in the Mediterranean was soon overshadowed by grim news. While cruising toward Tripoli on Nov. 24 Constitution was hailed by HMS Amazon which passed on the news that Philadelphia had become grounded chasing a ship into the Tripoli harbor and its 302 man crew had been captured.

Bainbridge (commanding Philadelphia) was a magnet for misfortune. He had overcome the professional disgrace of having the George Washington commandeered by the Dey of Algiers for the voyage to Istanbul. And earlier he had commanded the Retaliation and surrendered it to the French off of Guadalope in 1798 (in the quasi-war with France.)

The Tripoli grounding resulted from the aggressiveness that Jefferson had sought and that Preble demanded. But Bainbridge's navigating and ship handling displayed little more prudence than when he had anchored the George Washington within easy range of the Dey's gun batteries in Algiers.

Preble had dispatched Philadelphia with Vixen to Tripoli to relaunch the blockade. On Oct. 22 two weeks after their arrival on station, Bainbridge ordered the smaller Vixen to confront two corsairs in waters off of a nearby island.

Philadelphia was left alone to blockade the port, which sits on a shallow bay scattered with reefs and shoals. The anchorage for the Barbary fleet was far into the tight harbor behind a mole that protected the harbor from storms.

At 9 am on Oct. 31, Bainbridge spied a ship running close to shore, attempting to avoid the US frigate and safely reach the harbor to the West. He gave chase. Two hours later the Philadelphia had closed within firing range. But Bainbridge knew the ship was in shallow water. He ordered three leadsman to call out soundings.

A half hour later as the xebec glided safely into port Bainbridge turned to exit the harbor and almost immediately ran aground. For several hours the ship's officers and crew worked to get her off of the rocks. A boat was lowered over the side and found that deeper water was astern. Bainbridge backed the sails, but the ship didn't budge. He lightened the ship by offloading water, anchors and most of the ships guns. This too was to no avail.

In the meantime, Tripolitan gunboats had reached the Philadelphia and were peppering the ship from all directions. At 4 pm

Bainbridge assembled the ships officers. As he recalled the meeting later, "…every hope was fled of our being able to get her off, and not the least power whatever of injuring our enemies, and saw no alternative but our eventually becoming prisoners to Tripoli".

Bainbridge struck Philadelphia's colors just before sunset, a decision agreed to unanimously be the ship's officers, but decried by many among the crew. The carpenter was ordered to bore holes in her bottom to scuttle her, and secret codes and ammunition were ordered destroyed.

In preparation for a long captivity, the officers and crews donned all of their clothes and tried to hold on to their belongings. This was for naught as the Tripolitans stripped them of most of the clothes on their backs.

Sailing Master William Knight recounted being led to the castle where "arraing'd before Bashaw" the officers were treated better than they expected. However the officers' treatment was far better than the crew's. Soon it would worsen for all of them, when Preble's ships arrived to confront the Bashaw.

Bainbridge was faulted by crew members for surrendering, but also for his seeming indifference to their treatment in captivity. Seaman Elijah Shaw recounted the daily routine of the crew. They spent the night "ironed down to the stone floor" and were released in the morning, when they received their daily ration of a biscuit of ground beans and barley, a three ounce piece of goat's meat and vegetable oil. Two weeks into their captivity they were assigned to work parties hauling bags of sand and rock for a defensive wall being around the city. About 40 men formed a team to haul a cart filled with two to four tons of stone about ¾ of a mile. They were driven forward by a guard team of twelve "turks" and six drivers who used their whips with "an unsparing hand", Shaw wrote later.

Bainbridge passed time early in his captivity writing lengthy letters lamenting the ship's capture and defending his conduct in commanding her. His first correspondence to Preble laid responsibility for the capture on the commodore's decision to dispatch the schooner Vixen. In fact, a more cogent explanation of the cause was Bainbridge's aggressive pursuit of the xebec into the poorly charted and reef-filled harbor.

Within two days the wind had shifted and the Tripolitans were able to get the Philadelphia off of the rocks. In a letter to Preble from the officers' prison (the former US Consular House), Bainbridge offered precedents to his actions in his defense, "...we feel some consolation in knowing that it is not the first instance where ships have been from necessity (of running aground) oblidged to surrender, and afterwards got off by the enemy, which could not have been effected by the ships company; ---witness the Hannibal at Algesiras, the Jason off St. Maloes, and several others."

Bainbridge's letters soon were drafted with a better purpose. He began a regular flow of intelligence to Preble on troop and naval strength, force positioning and the mood of the captors. Some of the more meaningful intelligence was conveyed in invisible ink. The letters were forwarded on by the captives' constant friend and benefactor, Nicholas Nissen, the Danish Consul. In his first report from Tripoli, Bainbridge noted, "Mr. Nisson the danish Consul has been extremely attentive, & kindly offers every service of assistance."

Nissen came upon the books from the library of the captured American frigate in the city market, bought them and delivered them to the officers' house. With the books, Bainbridge established a school teaching the junior officers and midshipmen navigation and seamanship, which continued throughout their captivity.

In fact, Nissen was so attentive and supportive to the Americans he later was recognized by Congress, in a resolution noting his having supplied them with "provisions and bedding from his own house."

Official judgment of Bainbridge's conduct during the capture didn't come until after the war. A court of inquiry (comprised of three naval officers) took evidence from many of Bainbridge's officers. After these hearings they ruled Bainbridge blameless in the incident, saying that "no degree of censure should attach itself to him from that event."

The Philadelphia's capture slowed the momentum of the war. Respect for the nascent American state had been rising as word of Preble's aggressiveness spread. Suddenly the Bashaw's arsenal had a new weapon of great potential, plus 302 American lives to ransom.

Preble decided to postpone his arrival in Tripoli while he first established a base of operations for the winter in the Sicilian port, also named Tripoli. With the difficulty of operating along the North African coast a close-in base harbor like this was a necessity. The city's governor offered a hearty welcome: Sicilians had been battling back and forth with the Barbary states for centuries.

From there Preble conveyed the news of the capture back to Secretary of the Navy Smith. Preble refrained from judging Bainbridge's leadership but instead relayed Bainbridge's own account, "you can form as correct a one from Capt. Bainbridge's own letters of the 1st and 6th ulto, as it is possible for me to ---" he advised Smith.

Preble advised Smith that the capture "…very much changes my plans of operation for the present." He requested reinforcements of one or two frigates for the blockade, plus another to position near Gibraltar to free up the smaller Argus for coastal work. He also ordered a four-month supply of rum, winter blue uniforms for the ship's crew, salt pork, beef, bread, molasses and peas or beans. Preble planned to sail for Tripoli in the morning for an extended cruise, but noted that winter storms would doubtless prevent a continuous blockade.

Multiple copies were made of Preble's communiqué to be sent to Washington on different ships hoping to effect a quicker delivery. One was borne by Midshipman Christopher Gadsden for delivery in person to Smith. Transatlantic communication in the age of sail was glacially slow and woefully unpredictable. The Philadelphia was captured on Oct. 31, 1803. The event was reported to the U.S. Government in Preble's communiqué dispatched on Dec. 10. It was received in Washington more than three months after it was written and 4 ½ months after the ship's loss. Congress received Preble's report one day after Jefferson did. With it they were given the President's endorsement of the proposal to strengthen the Mediterranean fleet and urging the legislature to "enlarge our expenses in the Mediterranean."

Almost immediately after news of the Philadelphia's capture reached Washington it was made public. Several of Bainbridge's letters ran in the (Washington) National Intelligencer newspaper in March and April, 1804.

The financial strictures were still in place. But Congress passed a measure within six days to strengthen the Mediterranean force (reacting in part to public outrage at the Philadelphia's capture). The National Intelligencer announced the measure on March 23 in a story headlined with the famous phrase: "Millions for Defence, But Not a Cent for Tribute". The Navy was authorized to add two additional frigates to the fleet and to hire as many gunboats as necessary to the task.

With passage came a new special 2½ % duty on imports into the U.S. The measure was to be left in place until three months after ratification of a treaty ending the Barbary conflict. Treasury Secretary Gallatin's efforts to shrink the federal debt enjoyed strong support in Washington. Gallatin had a big voice in creation of the special fund, which insured that the war was paid for as it was fought, not later.

The Mediterranean Fund tariff remained in place for 4 ½ years. It brought in $4,408,344.67, according to a report from the Treasury Department to Congress and the President dated Feb. 15, 1810. Unexpended funds from the Mediterranean Fund were later used to build up the Navy.

Command and control of military operations in the circumstance faced by the United States in this conflict was an illusion. Jefferson led best when he sent commanders to North African waters with clear guidelines and parameters and the flexibility to maneuver within them. Preble flourished in such circumstances. By the time the capital knew of the Philadelphia's capture, his squadron had carried out a bold counterattack.

Chapter VIII

Preble established the squadron's base at the port of Syracuse on the Eastern coast of Sicily. He explained in a Dec. 10 report to Secretary of the Navy Smith that Marcello De Gregorio, the local governor, was particularly welcoming. He gave the Americans use of an arsenal and storehouses for supplies. He also offered the opportunity to buy fresh meat, vegetables, fruit, candles and rice "cheaper than they can be purchased in America."

Preble quickly headed to Tripoli to deliver money for the captives' care. They also reconnoitered the harbor's defenses and checked out the Bashaw's demeanor. Preble knew the dangers of winter cruising off Tripoli's shoals in Northerly winds, particularly the risk posed to Constitution, the squadron's sole remaining big ship.

Preble was joined off of Tripoli by the Enterprise, commanded by Stephen Decatur. The additional ship was effective quickly. On Dec. 23 it chased down and captured Mastico, a 64 ton ketch. Mastico flew Turkish colors, but it carried two Tripolitan officers and 10 soldiers, plus 42 black slaves. Preble ordered it taken to Syracuse as a prize. Some of the Tripolitans were identified as being among the group that sacked the Philadelphia (by an Italian doctor who had been in Tripoli when she ran aground).

Enterprise escorted Mastico to Syracuse where her papers could be translated from Arabic. Ten days later Preble wrote the Bashaw's Prime Minister proposing to exchange Mastico's crew for a like number of the captives from the Philadelphia.

From Syracuse, Preble began other diplomatic forays at buying the release of the American captives. At the same time, a plan to attack and destroy the Philadelphia before it could be used against American shipping was drawn up.

An early estimate from Lear of ransom costs for the crew (along with the purchase of peace) was $450,000. But in a report to Madison, Lear labeled that figure "certainly too high", noting a previous range of ransoms collected by the Bashaw of $500-600 per captive.

Some initial bargaining took place through intermediaries during the winter, but these never became serious. At one point Preble reported rumors that the Bashaw was seeking $3 million for peace and as ransom of the 307 Americans (almost $10,000 per man). "I presume our government will never accede to anything extravagant as we shall by that means hazard a war with all the Barbary powers by stimulating their avarice," he wrote.

In the meantime novice American diplomats posted overseas solicited the help of their host governments. In France, Russia and Sweden they asked respective foreign ministers to bring pressure, directly or through Istanbul, on the Bashaw. US Minister to France Robert Livingston excitedly reported to Preble a positive response from his French counterpart. Livingston acknowledged that he was completely unaware of the US government's desires, but pushed Preble to get local French emissaries to plead the American case to the Bashaw.

In fact, Jefferson was harshly critical when he learned of these pleas to foreign powers. He became infuriated after considering it for a few days. At first the President wrote Madison that he was "sorry" for Livingston's "asking the interference of France" with Tripoli. Two weeks later, he was enraged, calling the pleas "sordid" and a "national stain". He also pointed out to Madison the hurdles the diplomats were placing in the path of Preble's military efforts to subdue Tripoli. If the prisoners were released, Jefferson wrote, "what is the Commodore to do? To go to beating their town about their ears immediately after they have done us voluntary justice would be an outrage…"

Jefferson concluded that the US government would have to rely on Preble to decide on how to handle a situation in which "two inconsistent plans are going on at the same time…"

The plan for the Philadelphia had three different sources, including the captives themselves. Bainbridge had written Preble about weekly since his capture, but all of the letters had been held up (along with most other mail to and from the US squadron) in the offices of Jospeph Pulis, of Malta, who had been hired as the US representative there. (Preble quickly replaced Pulis, noting he "was formerly Consul to the Bashaw of Tripoly, has no respectability attached to his character---cannot speak a word of English And is by no means a proper representative for the US to have on the island."

Preble's lack of response to the letters understandably unnerved Bainbridge. But he kept writing, offering a wealth of good intelligence encoded or written in invisible ink. Along with reporting on the prisoners' treatment, Bainbridge described the exact location of the Philadelphia in the harbor, and the arrangement of defenses around her. Finally, he suggested a crew from the squadron enter the harbor with stealth and burn her.

With the discovery of the waylaid mail, six of Preble's letters in response were received by Bainbridge in mid-February. Bainbridge thanked Preble for his strong assurance of (Preble's) "exertions to relieve our distresses, and effect our release from bondage."

While Tripoli's maritime skills may not have been sufficient to make use of the Philadelphia, Preble was concerned that the ship would be sold to a larger Barbary state. Around the same time that Bainbridge submitted his suggestion of setting fire to Philadelphia the same idea came from Lt. Stephen Decatur, and apparently into the mind of Preble himself independently.

The plan that coalesced was for an American assault group to sail surreptitiously into Tripoli. They would quickly board the Philadelphia, subdue her Tripolitan defenders, set her ablaze and escape. The plan required three ingredients. Through good planning or good fortune, Preble possessed all three.

First, a pilot experienced with Tripoli's treacherous harbor, Salvatore Catalano, was recruited in Malta. Catalano also possessed a valuable language skill, fluency in the linguistic brew of Arabic, Turkish and Italian, that was the linqua franca of the Mediterranean.

Next was an enthusiastic group of volunteers to carry out the mission. Preble's leadership and the daring men who had been attracted to the fledgling Navy made that likely. In fact, Decatur's call for volunteers was oversubscribed, with about double the required number of men stepping forward.

The final essential element was the Mastico. Renamed Intrepid by Preble, this ship was ideal for the attack. Her silhouette looked like a Mediterranean trading vessel, not an American man-of-war.

Preble issued orders to Decatur (commanding Intrepid) and to Charles Stewart (on Siren) in Syracuse on Jan. 31, to take ammunition for Philadelphia's 18 inch guns in the hope they would have time to fire on the Bashaw's castle, along with the fuel necessary to set her afire before disembarking. Stewart was told to change Siren's rigging and the color of her sides, and to cover her gun ports so that she appeared a merchant vessel as she lingered off shore in readiness.

Preble picked an extraordinary mission leader in Decatur. The son of the captain of a revolutionary privateer, Decatur had been taken to sea by his father as an eight-year old boy. He attended the University of Pennsylvania. His nautical training came from John Barry, one of the founding captains of the revolutionary American Navy.

The two ships sailed for Tripoli on Feb. 2. Before departing, Midshipman Ralph Izard wrote his mother back in Charleston, South Carolina: "Before this day (a week hence) I am in hopes we shall have the happiness of seeing the Philadelphia in flames --- we shall astonish the Bashaws weak mind with the noise of shot falling about his ears. Perhaps some shot 'more lucky than the rest may reach his heart' and free our countrymen from slavery."

The two ships approached the coast of Tripoli on Feb. 7. They were separate and appeared unrelated. The latteen-rigged Intrepid looked like routine traffic along the shore of North Africa. The Siren appeared like a small European merchant ship.

But on their arrival the weather quickly turned foul. Navigating the shoal-laced coast in a winter storm was way too risky so they headed back to sea. For seven days the ships rode the heavy seas of a severe winter storm. The 74-man crew of Intrepid was jammed together on a vessel of only 70 tons or so. Catalano and the six midshipmen all spent their nights, if not on watch, trying to grab sleep on a platform positioned atop the ship's water casks.

Intrepid and Siren became separated during the storm and when the weather improved, Intrepid reached the waters off Tripoli first. Decatur decided to proceed with the attack without Siren lest the improvement in weather reverse. As the ship neared the harbor only Decatur, Catalano and six crew members were on deck and they were all costumed in the garb of North African seamen.

Siren had caught up and was just offshore when Intrepid entered the harbor. The password was given to the attacking crew: "Philadelphia", and British colors were aloft. The crew had rehearsed the plan of attack repeatedly before the storm, but Decatur worried whether they were still sharp after the hiatus.

The harbor was quite still at 10 pm as they approached the captured frigate. Decatur saw two cruisers off Philadelphia's quarters and two gunboats off of her bow. As Intrepid drew closer, a voice on the captured frigate broke the silence warning them off. Catalano responded with a ruse. He explained that his ship had lost its anchor in the storm and requested permission to tie up alongside for the night.

An interchange followed with the Tripolitans asking about cargo and ports of call and Catalano responding with reassuring (and false) details. Queried about Siren, Catalano identified her as a Tripolitan merchant just in from Malta.

As Intrepid drifted close in the wind died. Calmly Decatur ordered out a ship's boats to carry a line to Philadelphia to pull them in. Finally, when the Intrepid was a few feet from Philadelphia the Tripolitans guarding her realized they had been duped. Shouts of "Americanos" arose, but it was too late. The American boarding party was leaping between the ships. Decatur jumped first, but his foot slipped momentarily. A young Midshipman, Charles Morris, was first to land.

Once on board the Americans encountered feeble resistance. From the four nearby boats "we rec'd no annoyance," Decatur later reported. About 20 Tripolitan sailors were killed with cutlasses, knives and pikes during the attack and a "large boat full got off, and many leapt into the sea," Decatur reported. The Americans --- following their well rehearsed plan --- spread out in groups. They lit fires in the gunroom, storerooms and several vulnerable spots on deck. The groups gathered together on the spar deck as flames began to shoot from the holds. The melee on the frigate awakened much of the town which looked out to see their captured prize burning fiercely.

Shouting from the decks of the Philadelphia spread far across the water, even to the American captives who rejoiced at the sight. Bainbridge called it a "most sublime sight". The Bashaw also witnessed much of the attack, according to Nissen, "the Bashaw saw the whole business with his own eyes ---the fire ship was burnt beyond reach before they could give orders," he reported later.

As the fires burned, the boarders cut the lines to Intrepid and jumped aboard her. Decatur escaped last after Philadelphia's destruction was a certainty. But a safe escape was still far from assured. The Intrepid was still loaded with combustibles and the Tripolitan shore batteries were manned and firing. Intrepid moved slowly out amidst the firing, towed by two boats with crewmen pulling on the boats' oars. The shore batteries' firing was ineffectual, with their shots falling wildly across the harbor, with only one shot ripping through Intrepid's top-gallant sail. Then the Philadelphia's guns (loaded by the Tripolitans for her defense) went off sending shot in all directions.

Now a new gale was approaching from the North. The boats towed Intrepid into its path. But the ship raised sails and took in its boats before the storm hit. The attack had been a great success. No Americans were killed and only one was slightly wounded.

Philadelphia burned on through the night, eventually drifting right under the walls of the Bashaw's castle. At 6 am the next day, Lt. Charles Stewart, commanding Siren, could still see the glow of the fire from 40 miles to the North as they steered back toward Syracuse.

The American captives celebrated, but soon were placed under greater scrutiny. The ship's surgeon, Joseph Cowdery, maintained a journal in which he recorded the attack and aftermath. The next day, he reported, "the Turks appeared much disheartened at the loss of their frigate. A strong guard was put at our door, and we were forbid going out" (even to tend to the sick in Cowdery's case).

Decatur and his party were lauded on their arrival in Syracuse. Preble signaled: "Have you succeeded?" as soon as he saw the ships approaching. "Yes" came the response from Siren. No qualification to the response was needed.

Surprisingly the success of the mission became the focus of a dispute some 20 years later, and from an unlikely source: Decatur's wife Susan. Newly a widow and short of funds, she filed a claim for prize money for Philadelphia. She argued that Philadelphia could have been recaptured rather than destroyed in which case Decatur would have earned prize money.

In official Navy hearings, those present in the attack weighed in on both sides of the debate. However, the argument was mainly about her claim for compensation. Decatur's orders were explicit and he executed them flawlessly.

Chapter IX

Preble knew he needed greater force to mount a real attack on Tripoli. His squadron was lacking the flexibility of moving guns close to shore without risk from the reefs and shoals. So Preble mounted a diplomatic campaign to buy or borrow gunboats and bomb ketches from a friendly Mediterranean navy.

Preble eliminated several possibilities before settling on Naples and Sicily. He assumed their shared enemy in the North African state would draw a sympathetic hearing for his request. He was right. On April 17, James Cathcart delivered the request to Lord Acton, the Neapolitan king's Prime Minister. Acton offered the loan of gunboats and mortar boats fully equipped and armed.

Preble hadn't been authorized to hire or buy vessels, but clearly believed that Jefferson's impatience for military progress gave him latitude in moving ahead. Eventually Acton and the Sicilian king acceded to Preble's request, generously giving the American squadron a new set of tools. Naples even delivered the vessels manned, with the Americans only responsible for the crew's pay.

Meanwhile, Tunis began to threaten the Americans from the West. The Bey doubtless perceived American weakness because of the 300 prisoners held in Tripoli. He also had complaints that revolved around Tunisian vessels caught up and seized in the Tripolitan blockade.

Preble's squadron became a presence off of Tunis throughout the spring and early summer of 1804. They gathered intelligence and bargained with the Tunisians.

The fleet's presence, particularly that of Preble's Constitution, seemed to give pause to the Tunisians as they issued veiled threats to American merchants. When Preble arrived on April 5, George Davis – the new American diplomat on station – advised Preble of a "menacing" conversation he had with the Bey.

Demanding compensation for captured property, the Bey offered an alternative: "I have the power to capture your vessels and pay myself," he warned. Preble responded that the Bey's threats were based on a frivolous pretext . His direction offered through Davis was: "On your answer will depend my future movements with Naval force under my command."

In fact, Preble's naval force was barely adequate to contain Tripoli and he was hoping to go on the attack against that city's fortifications. "I am at a loss for a sufficient number of vessels to blockade Tripoly and Watch Tunis," Preble recorded in his diary on board Constitution on April 17.

Preble was focused on Tunis based on his visit there 12 days earlier. In a report to Secretary Smith he noted "....everything was quiet, but the Bey is fitting all his cruisers & threatens to take our vessels if he is not in six weeks paid for the property captured by Commodore Morris' squadron."

On April 27, a pair of diplomats --- Davis and Richard O'Brien --- negotiated with Sapatopa, the Bey's Minister, who repeated the Bey's demand for a frigate from the US. He noted that Algiers had been granted a vessel. The Americans noted their annual payment of $8,000 in tribute to Tunis. "This is a small sum for our friendship," Sapatopa responded, according to the Americans' report to Washington. He added, "You have been three years at War with Tripoly; who has not the power that Tunis has --- You have spent Millions & done nothing --- You have lost a Frigate and her Crew --- You are tired of the War and want peace."

Davis and O'Brien responded forcefully (given their circumstances), "We have used but a small part of our force against Tripoly; his Corsairs have been shut up these 3 years and his port blockaded. We have spent much Money, and will spend more: the loss of the frigate was an accident --- but we have burnt her in a port called very strong. We repeat, that, our system is Peace and will continue the War to obtain it—".

In the end Davis paid $10,000 in settlement of Tunisian claims. The Tunisians continued to issue demands as part of the "system of Barbary". But the immediate Tunis crisis passed due to Preble's squadron appearing frequently in that harbor, and Tunisian nervousness about coincidental war threats from Russia.

But Tunis also eyed developments in Tripoli attentively: "There is also a strong motive, why His Excellency, should at this time, be indecisive, in treating with the U. States," George Davis, US Charge D'Affaires in Tunis, wrote Preble. "He waits the result of your summer campaign, against Tripoli..... it must be dreadful to Barbary ---or, we shall ever, bow the neck, and receive the tribulatory yoke, of half a dozen Pirates---".

As Preble prepared for a new assault on Tripoli, he also carried on a convoluted negotiation with the Bashaw to end the war. French Consul Beaussier was engaged in the negotiation based on Livingston's appeal in Paris. But Preble was suspicious of the French diplomat from the outset. Beaussier foresaw an expensive peace, "... the Bashaw's pretentions will be at least 500,000 dollars," he predicted in a March 28 letter to Preble.

Beaussier claimed to have used the threat of a potential American alliance with Hamet, the Bashaw's brother who he had deposed to assume his post, as a bargaining ploy. (This plan had been bandied about American diplomats and naval officers back to the days of Commodore Morris.) Beaussier reported that this and other claims of American tenacity had no effect on the Bashaw.

Hearing this Preble concluded that the French diplomat's sympathies tilted toward Tripoli, and that the only trustworthy European diplomat in Tripoli was Nissen, the Dane who had assisted the American prisoners. Preble's judgments about Beaussier and Nissen were reinforced by correspondence from Bainbridge who had observed their activities as they each related to the Tripolitans.

In June, Preble sent O'Brien ashore with an offer of $40,000 ransom plus $10,000 in payment to Tripolitan officials who "forward (US) views". In addition to the relatively small amount offered, O'Brien's approach was quite abrupt.

He engaged in little of the foreplay that was customary. This brought a quick and defensive rejection from Tripoli. Immediately, Beaussier wrote Preble advising that it was "not decent" to involve France in a ransom that was so insignificant.

One day later, Bainbridge's communication (written in invisible ink) informed Preble that Beaussier would not provide services against Tripoli's interests. He also advised a more patient negotiating stance: "Whoever negotiates should remain on shore, and take (the Tripolitans) in the time when they appear in the best humour."

At the same time diplomat Tobias Lear directed Preble to offer $180,000 in ransom (with no added payment for peace). Preble ignored this. As he reported to his boss, Secretary Smith, "I am confident was I to make the offer it would be accepted immediately, but it would be imprudent to offer a sum which would stimulate the avarice of the other Barbary powers." Preble clearly had observed the interconnected pattern of negotiations with the Barbary states more carefully than Lear, and was willing to ignore his direction.

He yearned to mount another attack on Tripoli, but patiently awaited the delivery of the borrowed gunboats and bomb vessels before taking the offensive again. In the meantime, the squadron maintained a blockade while Preble negotiated and maintained a display of force off of Tunis. He also was awaiting transfer of gunboats and bomb ketches to his command. Finally, in late July the Constitution headed South from Malta with the gunboats and bomb ketches in tow.

The plan was to move from blockade to attack, but Preble was guarded in his expectations. "I shall attack the Town & Harbor immediately after my arrival and hope to succeed in bringing the Bashaw to an honorable place," he wrote colleagues as he set out. "I have long been expecting a reinforcement to the squadron and have been extremely anxious for an arrival from the U.S."

Foul weather forced the squadron away from Tripoli soon after their arrival along that coast. They returned there on Aug. 3 and Preble immediately directed an attack. The maritime defenses of Tripoli included 22 gunboats (manned by 30-50 sailors each) as well as heavily fortified shore batteries equipped with 67 heavy cannons. The enemy gunboats had formed a line just off the mole which protected the harbor.

Preble's squadron bombarded Tripoli and its small fleet six times in the month long period beginning August 3. The first attack was the most effective. Preble's force consisted of the six borrowed gunboats and two bomb ketches plus the Constitution (46), Argus and Siren (8 guns each), Vixen and Nautilus (16 each), and Enterprise (14).

Stephen Decatur led one of the squadrons of gunboats in to attack Tripolitan vessels that were moored in a defensive posture near the harbor. His appearance caused them to retreat into the harbor. Decatur kept heading in toward a second group of Tripolitan defense boats. Capt. Decatur and his crew boarded and captured two and Lt John Trippe captured a third in the bloodiest man-to-man fighting of the war.

Stephen Decatur led a 19 man force that killed 16 men and wounded 19 on the first gunboat, which they attacked.

Capt. Decatur's younger brother, Lt. James Decatur, also commanded a gunboat in the attack. It came down on a fourth enemy gunboat and attacked at close range. Shortly after the attack began, the Tripolitans lowered their flag in a surrender, which turned out to be a ruse. As James Decatur led a boarding party on to the gunboat he was immediately shot in the head with a musket and plunged into the harbor. His crewmen retrieved him, but he died soon afterward when he was returned to the Constitution.

The American gunboats were outnumbered, but successfully withstood three attempts to encircle them. Covering cannon fire from the American brigs and schooners out of range of the reefs and shoals was essential to the gunboats remaining unscathed.

Meanwhile the two bomb ketches battered the town with shells despite, as Preble noted later in his journal, "...the spray of the sea occasioned by the enemies shot almost cover(ing) them...."

The Constitution exchanged fire with the gun emplacements in the Bashaw' castle and on the mole head battery. The ship was hit nine times during two hours of sustained fire. One shot came so close to Preble that it shredded his uniform before exploding on a cannon next to him.

After the battle that killed James Decatur, his older brother Stephen tracked down the Tripolitans that had fooled him with the fake surrender. Capt. Decatur assaulted the huge Tripolitan commander in charge of the gunboat and battled him. It was Decatur's sword against his foe's boarding pike. A wounded American sailor named Reuben Frank defended Decatur from a second attacker as the two wrestled on the deck of the gunboat. Decatur was wounded in the chest and arm and lost his sword in the fighting. As he was about to be run through he pulled a pistol from his pants and shot dead the man believed to have killed his brother. Later he wrote a friend about the day's battle, "I find hand to hand is not child's play, 'tis kill or be killed."

Preble was able to report an offensive success: three gunboats were captured and three were sunk. Forty-four men from the crews that manned these boats were killed. All of the American vessels survived the battle. Only James Decatur was killed and 18 Americans were wounded. In the wake of years of only partly effective blockades, and the daring, but defensive, destruction of the Philadelphia, this attack was a change of momentum. Unfortunately, as Preble hurried to continue the attacks through fair late summer weather, circumstances combined to cause the American this progress to falter.

The day after the attack, Preble prevailed on a French privateer running out of the harbor after taking on water to return with an offer to Sidi, the Bashaw's Prime Minister, of the return of 14 wounded prisoners to Tripoli where, he wrote, they "may be soothed by the presence of their friends" and be "furnished with fresh provisions and other necessaries which we have not on board." Preble added that he would "leave it altogether to the known magnanimity of his highness the Bashaw" whether American prisoners would be returned in exchange.

Preble attacked again four days later, concentrating on bombarding the mole, castle and town. While the American fleet blasted out a ferocious cannonade, the results fell far short of the first attack. Shells hit gun emplacements and fell through the town, but effects were negligible.

Worse, one of the captured gunboats, now manned by a 30-man American crew suffered a hit to a magazine. The gunboat exploded and 10 Americans were killed and six wounded. Whatever fear the first attack brought to the Bashaw was dissipated by the weakness of the second.

As the battle waned an American ship sailed into Preble's squadron. It was the John Adams; the lead ship in a group of five dispatched under orders drawn up after the Philadelphia's capture. The imminent arrival of this major force was what had Preble had hoped for. But Isaac Chauncey, in command of the John Adams, bore bad news as well. Two of the four frigates en route from America were commanded by men senior in rank to Preble. By naval tradition, the more senior of the two, Samuel Barron, would become Commodore upon arrival on station. This left Preble angry and discouraged.

Barron would arrive under Congressional authorization from 4 ½ months earlier. Congress had acted almost immediately upon learning of the Philadelphia's capture, including appropriating an additional $1 million for the war in 1804. Word hadn't reached Washington by then of the ship's destruction or of Preble's demeanor and other accomplishments.

Secretary of the Navy Smith's letter to Preble was dated March 11. It assured him of the administration's "high and unqualified approbation of your measures and your conduct." Had they actually known of Preble's "measures" and " conduct", it seems likely they would have found a way to leave him in command of some part of the Mediterranean force. (Preble expected Barron's arrival, but though they each would command separate squadrons.)

Once again knowledge in Washington was stale with the reality in the Mediterranean at a decisive moment. There was risk of a real slowdown in activity. But Preble's dynamism and professional attitude wouldn't countenance any pullback while he still was in command.

Preble didn't let on about his reaction to the news with the officers around him. But privately he was devastated. He acknowledged the seniority issue in an August 8 entry in his journal. But then he continued, "...how much my feelings are lacerated by this superedure at the moment of Vicotry cannot be described and be felt only by an Officer placed in my mortifying situation."

Preble worked to right this perceived wrong by bringing the war to a successful end while he still held command. He attacked and negotiated, then attacked and negotiated more. He wrote the US Naval Agent in Malta urgently ordering water and food. He noted the coming change of command and added, "I hope to end the War with Tripoli first and then the sooner (Barron) arrives the better as I am anxious to return home."

He resumed bargaining through French Consul Beaussier, using the imminent arrival of a much stronger force as a threat. "After their arrival it will not be in my power to offer a single dollar either as ransom or peace; as yet it is," adding a "final" offer of $80,000 for "ransom" and peace plus a $10,000 "consular present."

Beaussier quickly responded that the $90,000 was "inconsiderable". He said the Bashaw wanted to $200,000-$300,000. However he and Prime Minister Sidi thought a compromise of $150,000 was possible. The weaker second attack had also "encouraged" the Bashaw, Beaussier wrote. Preble upped the ante slightly to $100,000, but vowed that the destruction of Tripoli by the enlarged fleet was the only alternative.

In a separate note to Beaussier, Preble proffered a carrot: A $10,000 present "privately given" to Sidi for influencing the Bashaw to accept the settlement. This was coupled with a threat: Preble knew that William Eaton sailed with Barron's group intent on a land attack with the Bashaw's brother Hamet and his supporters. If there is no peace upon Eaton's arrival, Preble advised, "one of the frigates is ordered by the President of the United States to proceed to Alexandria to assist the Bashaw's brother.

Mr. Eaton our late consul in Tunis comes out in the frigate for that purpose, and brings our arms and ammunition, artillery and cash to enable him to regain the throne of Tripoly."

In fact, one day later Eaton arrived at Gibraltar on board USS President. In the meanwhile Preble had no favorable response to his offer and threat. So he watched the weather for fair conditions for another attack.

When the weather turned, he shifted to a night attack. Argus and Siren assisted by the gunboats towed the bombards in toward the harbor soon after sunset. They fired almost until dawn, hurling 300 shells into the city. The shelling slightly wounded the captive Bainbridge who had suggested the night attack in one of his invisible ink messages. His ankle and leg and leg were struck with building debris when a shell hit the fortress where he and the other officers were housed.

Three nights later Preble struck again at night, but with the whole squadron. Thirteen Tripolitan gunboats moved to capture the American gunboats. Constitution moved into the harbor quickly to defend the outnumbered smaller American vessels, which the Tripolitans seemed intent on boarding and capturing. Preble's flagship sailed with "tompions out, matches lit, and batteries lighted up, all hands at quarters, standing right in under the fort, and receiving a heavy cannonading from their battery," the purser of the John Adams later reported, describing it as "the most elegant sight that I ever saw." She sunk one of the Tripolitan gunboats and disabled two. The rested ran for safety.

The frigate spent 54 minutes in range of the Tripolitan shore guns and was hit 19 times. But it was to little effect, damaging sails but not the structure of the ship. Meanwhile the American squadron rained 600 rounds (at least 24 pounds each) on the city. The Americans suffered four dead and several wounded.

As August waned, Preble prepared for another attack. He had made repeated attempts to negotiate the prisoners' release and an end to the war to no avail. His urgency doubtless grew out of a recognition that his hopes of carrying the day were disappearing with fair summer weather and the approach of Barron's flagship.

In reality, the urgency and frequency of Preble's missives to Beaussier and the Bashaw made them counter-productive. The Bashaw perceived them coming from weakness, dug in his heals and upped the ante.

Beaussier even advised Preble that his eagerness to "parley" was "impolitic" and "detrimental" to American interests. "It had been much better at the beginning to have threatened, and to have followed up your attacks with energy and effect without entering into any negotiations," he wrote Preble on Aug. 29.

Danish Consul Nissen, a more trusted source in Tripoli, advised similarly in a Sept. 1 letter (written in lime juice) to US Consul George

Davis in Tunis. He observed that Preble "enters too often in parlamenting---the Bashaw takes it as necessity for peace and grows more obstinate. After each attack, there has been next day a flag of truce ---this is no good policy towards an enemy (such as) Tripoli."

Preble mounted another late summer attack of bombardment with the bomb ketches attacking the town and Constitution blasting away at the forts. Meanwhile the American gunboats maneuvered to attack Tripolitan gunboats. But as they got within range the Tripolitans retreated toward shore. At the same time, Preble planned what he hoped would be his most devastating attack. He planned to prepare the Intrepid as a fireship or "infernal". Stuffed with shells, explosives and wood scraps, infernals are sailed into attack at close proximity. It is then aimed at its target. The captain lights a fuse and he and the crew rush to escape by boat before the ensuing huge explosion.

Fireships had been used in naval battles for over 200 years, including most dramatically when six British fireships forced the Spanish fleet out of Calais harbor harbor in the battle of the Spanish Armada in 1588.

On August 31 work began to convert Intrepid to this use. She was loaded with 100 eighteen inch shells and 50 nine inch shells. The next day carpenters fitted her holds to be filled with 100 barrels of gunpowder.

Preble asked for volunteers for this dangerous mission. His invitation brought many more than the 13 required. Richard Somers was selected to command the 60-foot ketch, aided by officers William Harrison, Henry Wadsworth and Joseph Israel and ten crewmen from Constitution and Nautilus.

On the night of Sept. 3, Intrepid sailed away from the Constitution's anchorage and made her way through six miles of darkness to enter the harbor by its Western passage near the mole head battery, which she was set to destroy. Ten minutes after reaching the passage an awful explosion filled the skies for miles around the port.

Preble awaited the signal by flare the Americans had completed their mission and were returning by boat, but none came. In the morning, Nautilus, which had followed her in toward the harbor to within ¾ of a mile confirmed her destruction in a massive explosion.

The cause of the huge blast remains unclear. Some observers believe that Somers ignited the fuse to avoid capture. Others believed that she was hit by a shell from the mole head battery. Beaussier reported that the city itself and its fleet of vessels suffered no damage.

Afterward, Preble immediately began to wind down his attack. On Sept. 6, he dispatched Decatur to return the bombards and gunboats to the Sicilians in Messina. Preble wrote his expansive thanks to Lord Acton, Sicily's Prime Minister, describing Tripoli as a "powerful Barbary State".

Three days after dispatching Decatur to return the shallow draft vessels, USS President and Constellation finally arrived off of Tripoli. Barron had left from Hampton Roads on July 5, more than two months before. His arrival had been stalled by headwinds in the Atlantic crossing and in transiting the Mediterranean.

Preble was intent on heading home despite Secretary Smith's hope that he would continue the fight under Barron. Preble's strong desire was for independent command. Even more than Barron's posting as Commodore he chafed at the arrival at another Captain senior to him: John Rodgers, who was a much more difficult personality than the pliable Commodore Barron.

Preble's installation of a culture of boldness and discipline was strong and lasting on the youthful institution of the United States Navy. It was carried forward and built upon by many officers who had served in his squadron, including Decatur, Bainbridge, David Porter, Isaac Hull and Charles Stewart.

A scroll signed by officers who served in Preble's squadron makes clear the impact that he had on them. "We, the undersigned officers of the squadron later under your command, cannot, in justice, suffer you to depart without giving you some small testimony of the very high esteem in which we hold you as an officer and a commander." It was presented by Decatur, the new Commanding Officer of the USS Constitution.

Chapter X

Commodore Preble turned over his command just as William Eaton arrived in the Mediterranean bearing his plan to transform the American effort to include a ground attack. Ironically, Eaton was accompanied by military and diplomatic leaders who were skeptical of the plan, in marked contrast to Preble's enthusiasm for it.

Prior to Eaton's consular service in Tunis he had already established a colorful record of military service. He had served in the Revolutionary war, having enlisted from his Connecticut home just prior to his 16th birthday (by lying about his age). After the war, he went North to attend Dartmouth College, graduating in 1790 as George Washington formed the first government under the new Constitution. Two years later Eaton rejoined the Army, which was forming to fight Indian Wars in the Ohio Valley.

His campaign there presaged some of the tactics he would use in North Africa. Eaton had taken the time to learn some of the language of the Miami tribe, and to learn to blend into their surroundings. He had used those skills scouting the Miami tribe in 1793 and 1794. Then he had reported his findings to General Anthony Wayne, who commanded the fight in the Ohio Valley.

Eaton had acquitted himself well in the Indian wars there and in the South prior to beginning his consular duties in North Africa for the State Department in 1797. By an unlikely and inexplicable coincidence, Eaton had by then taken it upon himself to study the Koran and learn some Arabic. He had a strong desire to become knowledgeable in Middle Eastern culture and to see the Ottoman world up close. He had noted this interest in his letters and in journals, at one time recording: "I wish to learn Arabic and to find out all I can about the Ottomans. Some day I shall visit that far-off part of the world, and if the almighty wishes it for me, may even live there for a time. Therefore all I can discover and learn now will be of use to me later."

This wish was about to be fulfilled ten years later. Barely one week after Barron assumed command of the Mediterranean squadron,

Eaton laid out part of his strategy in an appeal for funding for Hamet's mission directed to Secretary of the Navy Smith. Eaton intended to launch the first step of the new strategy the next day --- an expedition into Egypt to find Hamet and join forces with him against Hamet's brother, the Bashaw.

Conditions for such an expedition couldn't have been much worse, with violent anarchy prevailing in Egypt and power divided amongst Ottoman Turkish troops, Mamelukes, marauding Arab bands and some British representation under that nation's Viceroy. Bringing Hamet out of Egypt and helping him build an invasion force was a daunting task.

Also, Eaton's own authority and his accountability were quite unclear. American power in the Mediterranean was divided between the Navy, led by Commodore Barron, and the State Department's Tobias Lear. Jefferson had given Lear the power to negotiate a peace treaty with Tripoli. Complicating matters further, Barron was incapacitated by illness and would soon pass off much military responsibility to the next senior Naval Captain in the squadron, John Rodgers.

In his missive to Smith, Eaton spelled out a variety of reasons to follow through on the long discussed mission, which had been viewed with varying degrees of skepticism by Lear, Barron, Rodgers and even Bainbridge (reacting in invisible ink letters from his captivity). For Eaton, one reason to carry out the plan trumped all others: He had already committed the United States to helping Hamet. "But to sum all considerations in one," Eaton wrote, "which ought to weigh down all the others, the faith of the United States is pledged to (Hamet) by letter from Mr. Madison to me…".

Eaton's journey into Egypt was postponed for nearly two months while he awaited a ship to carry him to Alexandria from Malta. During that time there was open conflict among the American leadership contingent over his plan. Lear weighed in against it in a Nov. 3 report to Madison: "I presume the cooperation of the Brother of the Bashaw of Tripoli will not be attempted. Our force is thought sufficient to compel him to terms without this aid, and in any event it is very doubtful whether he has it in his power, with any reasonable pecuniary assistance we might give to render us service."

In the end, Barron backed Eaton's plan to find Hamet and "if no other use can be made of him" help place him as the leader of Derne and Bengaze (two cities to the East of Tripoli).

Hamet and the Americans had engaged in a flirtation about an alliance for some time and this continued as Eaton went in search of him in Egypt. Hamet's "consul" wrote Barron on Nov. 1 introducing himself and asking for $10,000 in aid in taking Derne and Bengaze.

Eaton was deeply patriotic, but also sought fame and grandeur through his plan. As he set off for Egypt, he unilaterally advised his boss Smith of a broadening of his own role in the plan. "It is understood between Commodore Barron and myself that I am to accompany the Bashaw by land in the expedition against Tripoli next summer. This I shall cheerfully do on condition that he will give the inspection, field discipline, and disposition of attack and defense of his army to me ---".

Eaton and eight colleagues were delivered by the Argus to Alexandria on November 28, 1804, to head inland where, he noted "a state of general revolt renders traveling somewhat dangerous."

Over the winter Eaton spent his time in Cairo, Rosetta and Demanhour attempting to locate Hamet and act on the commitment for the military action, for which he had been soliciting American funds.

Eaton's journey up river to Cairo was made on "marches" (40 ton schooners) unique to the Nile region. Accompanying him were Marine Lieutenant Presley O'Bannon, two midshipmen, Richard Farquhar, two officials of the British Viceroy and a group of servants. The marches bore British and American flags. They were heavily armed as defense against the warring factions of Egypt: Arabs, mamelukes and Ottoman soldiers. Hamet had sought shelter among the mamelukes. Gaining safe transit through Egypt became his top priority.

They were surrounded by chaos. Landing at the village of Sabour on Dec. 6, Eaton reported on an attack there by Arab bandits. He considered interceding on behalf of the villagers, but for the "cool observations" of one of his British colleagues that what they witnessed were "common occurrences" and any relief they would provide "would be indeed but temporary". He analyzed the situation in Egypt in a letter to Sir Alexander John Ball, the British Civil Commissioner in Malta as follows: "Why this misery and spirit of revolution? from a despotic or rather a total want of Government! Egypt has no master: though the most frightful despotism. The Turkish soldiery, restrained by no discipline sieze with the hand of rapine, every thing for which passion creates a desire---".

The mamalukes, who dispute with these the right of domination, subsist themselves by means no much less oppressive, if more supportable and the wild arabs, availing themselves of the occasion plunder the defenceless wherever they can find plunder."

In late January, he received a letter from Hamet arranging a rendezvous just West of Alexandria. From there Eaton and Hamet began to build and outfit their invasion force. But first Easton advised Barron of the expanded role he had assigned himself for the expedition, having "taken command in chief of the Bashaws army and the directions of all operations by land."

But first he needed a force to command. He and Hamet began assembling a polyglot group to supplement their own forces. Despite Eaton's entreaties to Barron for 100 Marines, the American element consisted only of Lt. O'Bannon, Midshipman Paoli Peck, plus one Marine Sergeant and six enlisted men. The ranks soon were filled by Arab cavalry, Greek artillerymen and other mercenaries drawn from Alexandria's rich supply. The services of all of the mercenaries were procured on credit.

While Eaton's financial commitments began to outstrip what he had been authorized to spend, he optimistically projected the costs of the expedition would be paid for by the treasure taken as victors. Also, Hamet had committed any future tribute his government might earn from Sweden, Denmark and the Batavian Republic to Eaton for the U.S.

This was recorded in Article VI of a "convention" signed by Eaton and Hamet prior to setting off to dethrone the Bashaw. Eaton pledged "utmost extertions" plus "cash, ammunition and "provisions" to the cause of reestablishing Hamet as Bashaw.

In addition to moneys received from the three European states, Hamet promised to free the officers and crew of the Philadelphia. The convention named Eaton "General and Commander in Chief of the land forces. And if there were future wars between Tripoli and the U.S. both men committed their countries to treating captives not as "slaves", but prisoners of war entitled to prisoner exchanges without payment of ransom or tribute.

Eaton's planned advance was directed at an adversary weakened by the harbor blockade. In October, Surgeon Cowdery had observed "a great scarcity of grain" and noted a dispute between the Bashaw and Reis (Lisle), his son-in-law, over a stock of barley.

The US captive seamen were most affected by the shortages. Cowdery noted that for three days in October they had no bread. In December, they used a hunger strike to obtain bread and oil.

These shortages only partly deterred Tripoli. Hearing of the American move to install Hamet on a march from Egypt, his brother formed a force to march East to Derne and help defend it. There was substantial paranoia about the loyalty of the force though, as "the sons and nearest relations of the force's officers" were held in Tripoli, as "hostages for (their) fidelity" (as observed by Cowdery).

At the same time though, the Tripolitans pushed to negotiate a truce. The overtures came from their Foreign Minister Dhgies. Preble's attacks, the ongoing blockade, and word of a land force gathering in Egypt were having the desired effect on negotiations.

Rains continued to slow the advance of Eaton's party. He stopped for a day after 10 days' march, noting "incessant" rains plus thefts "by the Arabs" of ammo and guns. The thefts continued through the journey Two weeks later he'd greatly regret the lack of rain.

The expedition was a hard slog across a vacant and forbidding desert interrupted only by the threat of desertions recorded almost daily in Eaton's journal:

March 18: "I now learned, for the first time, that our caravan was freighted by the Bashaw (Hamet) only to this place, and that the owners had received no part of their pay. ----No persuasion could prevail on the to proceed to Bomba nor to wait our arrival thither for their pay.">

March 19: "The Bashaw paid off his caravan, who promised to proceed two days march a head. But, the same night, all except forty of them drew off for Egypt; and the others refused to proceed, leaving us in a perplexed and embarrassed situation..."

March 20: "Last night the rest of the camels left us to return to Egypt. ----I now discovered a complot between the chiek (sheik) Il Taiib and sundry other chiefs, at which I thought the Bashaw connived, purporting a resolution to proceed no further until they should have assurance of the arrival of our vessels at Bomba."

But Eaton persisted and pulled the sheiks and their followers in tow. The exact count of Eaton's army as the march continued is unclear as camel drivers departed, but bands of recruits joined up. Five days after having to lever the Bashaw out of a sit down strike, Eaton recorded in his journal the arrival in the party of "forty seven tents of Arabs (who) joined us with their families and moveables --- In this detachment are one hundred fifty warriors on foot."

The scant rations for the march so far (two biscuits and some rice per day) turned into only rice by the end of March. As rations and water decreased, revolt among the Arab tribesman loomed more seriously.

On April 8, more than a month into the march, Eaton left Hamet and his followers for a brief reconnoiter of the Mediterranean coast. When he returned he found Hamet's group encamped showing no intent to move forward. Later Hamet and his Arab supporters packed up to retrace their steps. Easton grew alarmed that the group would steal the few remaining provisions so he ordered "beat to arms". At that point an armed standoff took place.

Eaton recounted walking toward Hamet's force with "a column of muskets aimed at my breast." Some of the Bashaw's officers and some Arab sheiks intervened in his defense. A promise of a ration of rice ended the revolt, but not the hard feelings among this disparate troop. Eaton's account of the confrontation concluded: "We find it almost impossible to inspire these wild bigots with confidence in us or to persuade them that, being Christians, we can be otherwise than enemies to Mussulmen!"

By April 11, the Americans were cutting the buttons from their uniforms and exchanging them with the Bedouin women for fruit. The next day the last of the rice was dispersed, but eaten cold, hard and dry due to a lack of water. Despite these deprivations the troop marched 25 miles that day. The next day a camel was killed for food.

Fortunately the party was nearing Bomba, the rendezvous point with the Argus and its support ships, under the command of Isaac Hull, and their greatly needed supplies. But there was real (and understandable) paranoia that the rendezvous would not be pulled off. Crossing almost 500 miles of desert without guides and navigational instruments to arrive at the right place and time seemed a near impossible goal.

When the troop arrived at the sea near Bomba on April 15, no ships were in sight. The Americans were called "impostors and infidels". The Arabs decided to break off in the morning. Eaton, the Marines and the Europeans spent the night encamped high on a nearby mountain, hoping that the American ships would see their signal.

In the morning, one of the Bashaw's men joined them. He spotted a sail, which turned out to be the Argus. "Language is too poor to paint the joy and exultation which this messenger of life excited in every breast," Eaton recorded in his journal.

The Hornet arrived two days later laden with supplies. Eaton's group moved 22 miles to rendezvous with the ship at a harbor where landing the supplies would be safe.

Eaton updated his plan for the attack on Derne, based on intelligence that the town's defenses had been strengthened. Eaton petitioned Hull for cannons from the Argus, since needed artillery had not yet arrived, plus four barrels of gun power, and a proportionate number of flints and musket balls. He also asked that the guns of the Argus and the Hornet be available to bombard Derne from the sea.

Eaton's army resumed the march to Derne in high winds and rain. As they neared the city the landscape changed from the barren desert they had crossed to cedar trees and barley fields. The 500-man force that had set off from Tripoli to aid in Derne's defense was rumored to be closing in on the city. This complicated Eaton's attack plan. It also caused "alarm and consternation" among the Arab chiefs and "despondency" in Hamet, according to Eaton.

The next morning they refused to advance on Derne. Eaton finally convinced them with "much persuasion, some reproach" and the promise of an additional $2,000. Eaton's army camped on a hill overlooking the city and surveyed its defenses.

The fertile country around Derne was a respite on the forbidding coast of North Africa. It rested on the site of a Roman town with an old high wall marking its perimeter on the landward side. Shore batteries and a fort structure faced the steep, rocky seacoast.

Eaton joined a cavalry party scouting to gather intelligence for an attack. Here his ability to blend in with his Arab mercenary force kept him safe. The scouting party was able to sneak through an open gate into the city and return to camp with two prisoners.

Their interrogation revealed that the main body of reinforcements from Tripoli was only two days ride from Derne. They also learned of the disposition of the 1,100 men defending Derne, and of the eight cannons that defended the city from the sea.

The next day Eaton wrote the Governor of Derne asking permission to bring his troop and Hamet through the city, and to purchase supplies at a fair price. He concluded ominously, " I shall see you tomorrow in a way of your choice." The governor's response was less subtle, "My head or yours."

Nautilus had appeared in the Derne bay with two cannons dispatched by Barron for Eaton's use. Both were transported in to him by boat. After his men dragged one up the rocky precipice from the coast Eaton became concerned about losing "the favorable moment of attack" and left one cannon behind.

Eaton's strategy was for his forces to the attack the city from three Southerly directions in a pincer movement. The most heavily defended wall of the city (at its Southeast face) was assigned to the

Americans, European mercenaries and some Bedouins under the command of O'Bannon. The Tripolitan force under Hamet moved in directly from the South. The Arab cavalry was to ride to the attack from the Southwest. A reserve force comprised of the largest complement of fighters remained behind to be directed to the battle opportunistically where it could have the greatest effect.

While Derne's defenders had the advantage of good defensive positions, Eaton had superior force. Tribal additions to his impromptu force had swelled its ranks to 2,200 and the three American warships supplied firepower. The ships were placed for bombardment of the shore batteries and fort.

O'Bannon's force advanced toward the heavily defended Southeast wall of Derne. Hamet's troops, led into battle by a janissary named Selim, moved in from the South. O'Bannon's group was soon pinned down by heavy fire from the behind the city walls.

Around 2 pm fire intensified between O'Bannon's force and Derne's defenders. An accurate cannon shot from inside the city disabled the sole American cannon. Eaton feared the battle hung in the balance. He knew it would be impossible to regroup his ragged force once they were driven back. So he brought much of his reserve force to attack, ordering a charge on the city wall. As the charge reached the city, the defenders fled from their "coverts irregularly," Eaton recounted later, "firing from every palm tree, and partition wall in their way."

One of those bullets hit Eaton's wrist. But O'Bannon, the Marines, and a party of Greeks crossed through the town to the strongest battery. There they lowered the Tripolitan flag and raised they turned the cannons back on the remaining defenders of the town.

Hull had a clear view of this from sea: "At about half past 3 we had the satisfaction to see Lieut. O'Bannon and Mr. Mann Midshipman of the Argus with a few brave fellows with them, enter the fort, haul down the enemys flag, and plant the American Ensign on the Walls of the Battery, and on turning the Guns of the Battery upon the Town, they found that the Enemy had left them in great haste, as they were found primed and loaded at their hand."

Hamet's force had moved into the city during this turmoil and the Tripolitan troops were caught between the two forces. Within two hours Eaton's force had captured the entire town. One Marine had been killed in the battle and one wounded, who would later die of this wounds. Twelve others (including Eaton) were wounded less seriously and survived.

The next day Eaton sent two reports to Barron. The first recounted the battle. The second recorded its cost (including its prologue: the adventure in Egypt and the march across the desert from Alexandria). This made an extraordinary accounting. A force which reached 2,200 men covered almost 500 miles in 40 days and seized the city of Derne for a total cost of $30,000.

Chapter XI

Eaton immediately began to plan his defense of Derne from a certain counterattack from the Bashaw's forces based in Tripoli. At the same time, ignorant of Eaton's success, Rodgers and Lear received word of a serious offer by the Bashaw to negotiate peace. This entreaty came through the Spanish consul. In exchange for $200,000 the Tripolitans would release Bainbridge and his shipmates and end hostilities.

The Algerian regime had advised the Bashaw of Lear's presence near Tripoli and urged the Tripolitan leader to make peace quickly.

Lear termed the offer delivered by the Spanish "totally inadmissible", but knew that the $200,000 was an initial price tag, subject to dramatic change through negotiation. The Spanish predicted that face to face negotiations in Tripoli would produce a peace.

Word arrived shortly in the American headquarters in Malta of Eaton's incredible success. Lear, who had expressed great skepticism about Eaton's mission, was now quiet in response. But Commodore Barron (still severely ill and inactive militarily) knew that Eaton had greatly advanced the American cause. However, Barron believed that advance could only be made permanent through negotiation, not further attacks by Eaton and Hamet.

Barron had heard from Eaton about Hamet's volatility and his timidity in battle. He understood that such a leader would not conquer Tripoli and unseat his brother the Bashaw without American aid "far exceeding both the resources placed at my disposal and the powers vested in me by my instructions...", he later wrote.

Eaton's progress with Hamet in tow had a sobering effect in Tripoli. The captive surgeon Cowdery noted in his journal that the Bashaw was "much agitated" by an espionage report delivered to him from Malta. Three days later, after learning of the capture of Derne, the Bashaw's reactions swung wildly between cruelty and paranoia.. Cowdery noted in his journal a pledge by the Bashaw to kill all of the American captives. Then in contrast five days later Cowdery recorded his declaration that he would gladly sue for peace and release all prisoners without any payment.

In the meantime Eaton, aided by shore bombardment from Argus and Nautilus, successfully defended Derne and Hamet.

The Bashaw's forces attacked to regain Derna on May 16 at first light. They overran a smaller contingent of Hamet's cavalry posted in defense about 1 mile from the town. As they advanced on Derne and the local palace where Hamet was holed up, Eaton's forces fired from behind the walls surrounding the city, but the attackers swarmed through them on horseback. Finally fearing a rout, Eaton trained his cannons on attackers inside the city.

This had great effect: "Very fortunately a shot from one of our nine pounders killed two of the enemy from their horses in the courtyard of the palace," Eaton reported. "They instantly sounded a retreat, and abandoning the town at all quarters, were everywhere pursued by hamets cavalry until they were chased under the shot of the vessels, which galled them sorely in their flight."

The force of nearly 1,000 was driven back to their camp in the hills three miles from town. There they erected a defensive structure of stonewalls. Eaton sent a report to Barron on May 17. He explained his force's precarious situation and sought supplies, including rations, salt and ammunition.

Barron had been commanding from ashore in Malta, due to his ill health, in the hope the rest would cure him. This was to no avail. With barely sufficient energy to communicate, he yielded his post as Commodore to Rodgers as negotiations were about to commence.

Four days later Lear arrived off of Tripoli on board Essex with Rodgers accompanying him. They encountered a far weaker Jusuf. The blockade and bombardments had cut off much of the Tripolitan economy. As the negotiations began, Cowdery observed the Bashaw's sense of vulnerability from his financial woes and the alienation of his people.

The Bashaw released Bainbridge as a courier to deliver a solicitation for peace to Lear aboard the Constitution. Lear quickly agreed to negotiations in a message delivered by Lear to Sidi, the Tripolitan Foreign Minister.

At the same time, Eaton was encamped in defense of Derne. His forces and Hamet's engaged in skirmishes with "arabs". But bombardment intimidated the Bashaws's forces and the fighting ended quickly. The Bashaw's commanders "attempted to force the Arabs forward---They resisted and alledged, as on similar occasions, that they were willing to fight an enemy of their own mode of warfare; but they would not resist the Americans, who fired enormous balls that carried away a man and his camel at once, or rushed on them with bayonets without giving them time to load their muskets---".

As Eaton learned of Lear's negotiations, he realized his grand campaign was about to be cut short by Lear's negotiations with Tripoli. Eaton saw a treaty at this point as premature and a betrayal of Hamet (despite Hamet's recalcitrance as they crossed the Libyan desert). Eaton wrote Commodore Barron arguing that Lear's talks were dishonorable and unjust.

Eaton proposed instead to attack the enemy forces near Derne, and then march the 400 miles to Tripoli.

On June 11, Jusuf's forces again tried to retake Derne with a large cavalry attack lasting about four hours. Again, Hamet's forces, aided by the 12" guns of the Argus, drove off the attackers.

Eaton advised Hamet of the possible withdrawal of American support for his mission to retake the throne. On June 11, he conveyed Hamet's response to Barron as follows:

"He answers, that, even with supplies, it would be fruitless for him to attempt to prosecute the war with his brother after you have withdrawn your squadron from the coast----But without supplies he must be left in a most forlorn situation for he can command no resources here….."

In fact, American support for Hamet had been officially abandoned by a treaty signed by Lear one week earlier in Tripoli. All of the American prisoners were released and the hostilities ceased. In exchange, the Bashaw received $60,000. Bainbridge played an intermediary role in negotiating the treaty. His letter, read by Cowdery, informed the American prisoners of their imminent release. The surgeon reported they wept with joy. Still the harsh conditions of their captivity didn't end. "They were still drove to hard work, and many of them flogged."

Lear signed the treaty on June 4, 1805. Superficially it was quite simple. Both sides exchanged prisoners and the Bashaw was given $60,000 "for the difference" in the number of prisoners (300 Americans vs. 100 Tripolitans who had been seized in battle by the Americans). In addition to end the blockade and attacks American support for Hamet would cease. And the Americans were to work "to persuade" but not "use any force" to convince Hamet to withdraw from Derne. Hamet's wife and children, imprisoned by Yusuf, would be returned to him.

However, the American government was to learn in 1807 that Lear also signed a secret side deal that rendered the treaty far less simple and benign. The side deal cast great doubt on his trustworthiness and negotiating skill. (We will learn more of the side letter later.)

Lear wrote a brief explanation of the deal (but not the side letter) to Eaton on June 6. He credited the "heroic bravery" of Eaton and his American colleagues at Derne, which he said had made a "deep impression" on the Bashaw. Lear detailed his efforts on Hamet's behalf, but said that pressing that case too hard "might prove fatal" to the officers and men of the Philadelphia.

Lear's letter reached Eaton on June 13, delivered by Captain Hugh Campbell of Constellation. Eaton immediately advised Hamet of the treaty and the removal of support for their advance on Tripoli. Hamet decided quickly to depart with Eaton and Campbell. But he kept it a secret as he expected a revolt to occur when his troops received the news. New ammunition and supplies were sent ashore as if the mission would proceed.

Immediately, and very secretly, that night Eaton withdrew the Greeks (an artillery group), Hamet and his retinue of guards and servants along with the American Marines and Naval officers. Eaton boarded his own boat last. Just off the beach Eaton saw the troops who had supported his grand expedition and battle for Derne gathered on the shore and battery "some calling on the Bashaw (Hamet)---some on me---some uttering shrieks ---some execrations."

While Eaton viewed the peace as "more favorable" than any gained by the Europeans or Americans in the past 100 years, he lamented the abandonment of his allies at Derne. He also viewed the peace as "more honorable", an opinion he would change dramatically when he learned of Lear's side deal with the Bashaw. (Lear also claimed the deal with Tripoli as "highly honorable" when he reported it to Barron.

Eaton immediately requested passage back to the US on the first ship to depart from the Mediterranean squadron

Jefferson's satisfaction with the treaty was to dissipate quickly. As Eaton made his circuitous return trip through the Mediterranean and across the Atlantic, he bore an extraordinary plea to the President. In this letter, Hamet politely recounted Eaton's commitments to him.

There would be no peace "General Eaton assured me", Hamet wrote, "unless I was placed in my own seat (throne)...".

Hamet continued with a summary of their incredible adventure on the desert journey from Alexandria to Derne and in the ensuing battles (while omitting his vacillation with the mission and the many moments of subtle rebellion against Eaton).

With the surprising news of Lear's treaty, Hamet said he had received assurance his brother Jusuf "would restore his family" and that he also would receive a pension from the US government. Hamet said he expected his family "daily", but had recently been told by his brother Jusuf that he "would not let them go..." Hamet concluded with a plea: "I therefore fling myself on the mercy of your excellency, who, under the influence of just laws will not fail to rend me that justice which oppression and misfortune entitle me to."

Eaton had much opportunity to reflect on Lear's treaty by the time he landed in Baltimore on Nov. 5, 1805. The passage of time only increased his anger. Likewise his suspicions were raised about the continued captivity of Hamet's wife and family. He quickly traveled to Washington. Soon he was expressing his feelings with characteristic strength to Smith, Madison, and various Congressional leaders.

This all made for a politically charged environment when the treaty came up for ratification in the Senate on January 13, 1806. As such, it was subject to rancorous debate throughout the capital. This was fueled in part by a second pleading letter from Hamet, this one addressed "To the People of the United States of America." In grandiose prose reminiscent of Eaton's, Hamet again recounted his story up to the point of Lear's treaty with Jusuf. "At this junction a peace is concluded in which a Throne acquired by rapine & murder, is guaranteed to its usurper, and I the rightful sovereign, the friend and ally of America ... left unprovided for."

In the end, after three months of vigorous debate, the Senate confirmed the treaty by a vote of 21 to 8. There really was little choice, as no realistic alternative was available. By then a new closer and more powerful military threat to the US had emerged, and more specifically a threat to its shipping,. The issue of how to resolve any unmet commitment to Hamet lingered, however.

Prior to the vote, Eaton was lionized in several cities as he toured the country. The Massachusetts legislature awarded him 10,000 acres of timberland in its Maine district. As he learned more of Hamet's plight his journey home became more of a political protest of Hamet's treatment by the US government.

While Eaton's appearances in Washington and other cities didn't derail the treaty's confirmation, it did win him complete reimbursement of the $20,000 he had expended from his own pockets on the Derne assault. More symbolically Congress awarded Eaton a medal. Also, James Greenleaf Whittier wrote a poem wrote a poem memorializing the valor of Eaton and his colleagues.

After the peace with Tripoli, the Mediterranean squadron under Rodgers' command had grown to its greatest size to date. In this position of strength it faced its final confrontation.

During the blockade off Tripoli, Rodgers had captured a Tunisian xebec and two Neapolitan prizes the squadron had seized. The Bey of Tunis demanded the return of the three ships and implied hostilities as the only alternative. He also demanded a 36-gun frigate as recompense for the seizure.

In response, Rodgers assembled an impressive array of warships off Tunis, including five frigates. The Bey initially refused to negotiate with Decatur, who Rodgers sent ashore as his emissary. But the Bey quickly reconsidered and withdrew his hostile response even before it had been delivered.

While the military confrontation ended quickly, the diplomacy dragged on through 1806. It involved a passage to Washington aboard USS Congress for a Tunisian envoy, Sidi Suliman Melli Melli. The matter ended peaceably. With no blockade of Tripoli, Jefferson ordered the return of the ships to Tunis. Melli Melli gave the President Arabian horses for Monticello. However, the upright Jefferson (who routinely refused such gifts) ordered the horses be sold to pay for the expenses of Melli Melli's trip.

Melli Melli's trip ended with the Bey's written thank you to Jefferson for American hospitality extended to his envoy: "And finally, offering prayers for your prosperity," the Bey wrote, "I wish you from Heaven, my Great and Good friend the most complete felicity."

So the American conflict in North Africa under Jefferson ended with a powerful show of American naval force --- the greatest assembled in the conflict to date. And this show of force peacefully evoked a desired political result.

There still remained the matter of Hamet's wife and family. Dr. George Davis had been named to the post of Consul General of

Tripoli. In April, 1807, Hamet wrote Davis reminding him of the treaty's supposed promise of the return of his family.

Within five days of his arrival in Tripoli, Davis' pressure on Jusuf's government brought to light Lear's side deal with the Bashaw regarding Hamet's family. But Davis was successful in getting Jusuf to promise to release all of the members of Hamet's family who wanted to leave (one daughter had married in Tripoli and chose to remain behind).

In October, after Davis had arranged transit to Syracuse the group departed Tripoli. In November, Jefferson delivered a copy of Lear's secret side deal to the Senate.

The President also ordered a diligent reexamination of all of Lear's correspondence with the American government in search of some mention of this side agreement. None was found. Jefferson offered an inconclusive but damning judgment on the matter.

He wrote that he was uncertain whether this was due to a "miscarriage" or "failure of … ordinary attention and correctness…".

The withdrawal of the American squadron from the Mediterranean came quickly after the confrontation with Tunis. The circumstances under which it was ordered home presaged America's next great battle. Instances of impressments of American merchant seamen by the Royal Navy had been on the rise.

Then in June, 1807, the ongoing tension flared into aggression off of Hampton Roads, Virginia. HMS Leopard, a 50-gun man of war fired on the 40-gun American frigate Chesapeake, demanding that the American vessel muster its crew for inspection by the British who were looking for deserters from the Royal Navy. Captain James Barron surrendered Chesapeake without firing a shot. Three members of Barron's crew were killed and eight badly wounded in the British attack.

Barron's weak leadership drew the immediate censure by six of his own officers including the Chesapeake's First Lieutenant.

With attacks on the Virginia coast by the British Navy feared, on July 14 the Secretary of the Navy ordered the immediate return of the entire Mediterranean squadron to Boston. Smith specified Boston, he wrote, because it offered "less risk…. than (going to) any other Port in the United States."

As the United States edged its way to an appropriate place among nations, its neutrality in the war between Britain and France had placed it in a precarious spot.

Each of the great powers resented America's unwillingness to join in its fight, or at least wanted it to cease trade with the other. With peace prevailing in the Mediterranean American merchant shipping increased, making America's status in the conflict even more of an issue.

The Chesapeake affair underscored a particularly tense source of conflict with the British: the impressments of American sailors who the British Navy claimed were deserters from its ships. Seizing American sailors off of merchant ships was the cause of great hostility toward the British in the U.S., particularly in its seaports.

Jefferson knew that the US Navy could do little militarily to thwart these British seizures or to revenge them afterward. So he decided to rely on soft power: diplomacy, and then economic coercion. In 1806, Congress had passed the Non-importation Act, banning specific British products from American shores. Its intent was to give American diplomats in London pressing American trade and maritime rights a meaningful, non-military threat. The law had been in effect for only five weeks in 1807 when Congress suspended it for a month at Jefferson's urging. It was viewed as unenforceable and of dubious value as a bargaining tool with the British.

In December, 1807, Jefferson learned that the efforts by US diplomats to get the British to stop impressments had come to naught. In fact, the British had decided to expand impressments to include naval vessels as well as merchant ships. Quickly, Jefferson proposed to Congress even greater economic measures: a complete embargo on trade. Thereby no American merchant ships would be vulnerable carrying goods across the Atlantic. Jefferson also thought barring goods from reaching Britain would pressure their leaders to moderate the country's stance on impressments.

Naval strategy had shifted somewhat through the terms of all three presidents, largely due to the rise and fall of specific threats. With the winding down of the Mediterranean conflicts this happened again. The direction from the Jefferson Administration was toward a naval capability that was less global and more defensive.

This was a better fit for Jefferson and his party. They had been focused on reducing expenditures and government debt and avoidance of conflicts, particularly with European powers. And Congressional opposition to a wide-ranging naval fleet was even stronger than the President's misgivings.

With the apparent threats from Britain and France, the focus shifted to construction of gunboats and defensive fortification of the main Atlantic and Gulf Coast ports. In December, 1807, Secretary of the Navy Smith proposed to Congress the construction of 188 gunboats. The measure passed quickly with overwhelming support in both houses.

The construction of these vessels seemed to follow no apparent pattern or design. They were wide ranging in size and design, perhaps because their construction sites were broadly dispersed. Many could not be safely sailed on the seas out of sight of land. The gunboat program was later reviewed during the next administration (of James Madison). Most of the gunboats were inactive and Madison had abandoned his predecessor's strategy for their deployment. Jefferson's noted biographer, Dumas Malone, wrote: "Most of the money spent on gunboats now appears to have been wasted, but they appealed to Jefferson and probably even more to Congress on grounds of economy, and in this time of desperation they represented to him a desirable experiment."

Enforcing the embargo had proved a daunting task and one that the government never mastered. (There was even brisk smuggling at the North end of Lake Champlain to avoid the embargo.) More importantly, the economic woes caused by the cessation of trade made the embargo very unpopular, particularly in mercantile regions like New England. After much political lobbying including petitions and protest marches, Congress took up the matter as Jefferson's Presidency drew to a close. The Embargo was abandoned in favor of a Non-intercourse Act, which banned trade with Britain or France under equal terms. It allowed trade with all other nations. It took effect immediately after Madison assumed office (allowing time to notify traders, shippers and seamen of the change).

Jefferson's two presidential terms ended in March, 1809, with his Republican Party in the predominant position politically. James Madison, Jefferson's ally in many battles and closest advisor, won the election of 1808 handily.

This was in spite of devastation wrought on the national economy by the threats to American trade and neutrality coming from both England and France. Of course, the embargo instituted by Jefferson and the Republican Congress to apply economic pressure on England and France had also imposed severe damage to America's prosperity.

In fact, the weapon of trade restriction, which Jefferson had leveled across the Atlantic, had been turned back on the U.S. and had frozen American commerce. In the year prior to Madison's inauguration, American exports dropped by almost 80%.

Jefferson had battled doggedly for America's trading rights and for free use of the seas for that purpose. Ironically, as his decades of political leadership drew to an end, trade was dead in the water, blocked in some part by the U.S. government's own policies.

Jefferson's style of governing was one of simplicity. Conforming with that he celebrated the end of his presidency in a quiet manner riding down Pennsylvania Avenue with his grandson in Madison's inaugural parade. Soon after that he retired to Monticello. He was 65 years old and understandably worn out from two eventful and taxing terms as President.

Epilogue

When he left office Jefferson had to be disappointed with the end resultof his experiences at naval leadership. He had intended to secure American trading rights (in the Mediterranean in particular) and freedom of the seas as a pathway to American prosperity and economic strength. In fact, when Madison succeeded Jefferson as President, US trade was almost completely shutdown. Meanwhile, American ships were tied up in their own homeports up and down the East Coast by restrictions imposed by the Jefferson administration and Congress, as well as the threat from the world's great powers: England and France.

Progress toward a second strategic naval goal of the Jefferson presidency, strengthening the Navy into an effective force, was called into real question by the handling of the Chesapeake affair.

In fact, the Chesapeake affair did not represent the state of the Navy at all. The whole structure of naval leadership had benefited greatly from the example and teachings of Edward Preble, Jefferson's most notable military appointment. This became very clear upon the outbreak of the War of 1812. Early battles in this conflict made it quite clear that the Navy's officers had absorbed Preble's lessons: structure and discipline, frequent gunnery drills and decisive action in battle.

In the war's first (and namesake) year, three officers, who had served notably under Preble, achieved clear and marked success in battles with the Royal Navy.

First Isaac Hull, commanding USS Constitution encountered the 38-gun British frigate, which was en route from Bermuda to its station at Halifax, Nova Scotia. In an afternoon's battle in August, battered her and ultimately forced a surrender.

By the end of that notable year, United States, commanded by Decatur, had captured the 49 gun Macedonian, and William Bainbridge and Constitution had destroyed HMS Java (38).

The two remaining years of the war (1813-14) saw a balance of American and British victories. Never again though would American naval prowess be discounted to the degree it had been prior to 1812.

The American Navy ranged from the British Isles to South America disrupting British shipping. Most memorable was the expedition by David Porter, who took the Essex into the Pacific on Feb. 24, 1813 in search of British ships. He spent the next year disrupting a major British whaling operation off of South America. The British were forced to send a squadron of ships to hunt him down.

More than a year after the Essex entered the Pacific, Porter was forced to surrender her off of the coast of Chile. But this was not before he had seized or destroyed most of the British whaling operation. The Essex (one of the subscription ships) became the HMS Essex. Porter and the surviving members of his crew were allowed to return to the US in a companionship, having sworn to not fight as they returned home.The War of 1812 ended on Christmas eve of 1814 with the US and England signing the Treaty of Ghent. The agreement restored American interests and territorial boundaries to their pre-war state.

The Americans had surprised and embarrassed the great Royal Navy. However, the Americans by no means had emerged victorious. But in winning some notable battles the US Navy's capabilities had been established in the minds of its own people and in those of other naval powers.

Jefferson's gunboat strategy had been a detriment to the American cause. Like many naval weapons systems devised and promoted for political purposes, it served the needs of Congress and the President far better than it did the Navy.

The Treaty of Ghent made way for the US to settle a long-standing score with a British ally ---Algeria. This conflict had begun almost coincidentally with the War of 1812 with yet another complaint about tribute. The annual provision of military supplies from the US to Algeria had been going on since 1795. (It was the sole remaining tribute arrangement between the American government and a Barbary state.)

In July, 1812, Dey Hadji Ali refused an American shipment of gun powder and had demanded cash instead. Tobias Lear had become the US Consul General in Algiers. He refused the demand. In retaliation, the Dey ordered Lear out of the country, but would only allow him to leave upon the payment of tribute.

Two and one-half weeks after Lear delivered on the cash demand, the Algerians captured the American merchant brig Edwin out of Massachusetts and demanded ransom for its captain and 10 man crew.

Madison had a clear and strong intent to remedy this upon peace with England. Within one week of the Senate's February, 1815 ratification of the Treaty of Ghent, the President asked Congress to declare war on the Dey and Algiers. And only one week later Congress voted its approval.

Madison's naval deployment to the Mediterranean wasn't bound by the limits imposed on Jefferson by a small and infant Navy. While not yet a real naval power, Madison's navy had the firepower to extend real force across the Altantic.

Madison formed two squadrons and selected men familiar with the Barbary theater to command them: Bainbridge and Decatur. Decatur's squadron departed first with three frigates, Guerriere, Constellation and Macedonian. Accompanying them were two sloops, three brigs and two schooners.

After arriving in the Mediterranean on June 15, Decatur picked up intelligence of Algerian warships off of Cape de Gatt southeast of Granada. The squadron quickly headed off in search of them. Two days after entering the Mediterranean, a lookout on Constellation spotted Meshuda, a 46-gun frigate flying Algerian colors. Constellation was joined in the chase by Guerriere and the sloop-of-war Epervier. Once they closed on her, the Americans attacked ferociously. The Meshuda was commanded by the Algerian Navy's Admiral Reis Hammida. He fled Northeast toward Cartagena, Spain in an effort to escape the American attackers. But the sustained American attack wounded scores of Algerians and killed 30 including Hammida. After the American sloop Epervier blasted Meshuda at close range, the Algerians surrendered.

On June 28, Decatur's squadron arrived off of Algiers to demand an end to Algerian aggression and the return of enslaved American sailors. Two days prior to the squadron's arrival, the Epervier, plus an American brig and two schooners had chased down an Algerian brig. In the ensuing fight the Algerian brig ran aground and was captured. So the Algerian Navy had lost its commander, two ships and hundreds of sailors captured, wounded or killed within two weeks of the American squadron entering the Mediterranean. This allowed Decatur to deliver Madison's strong and just list of demands to the Algerian Dey . A letter from the President and another from Decatur and American envoy William Shaler spelled out the American's requirements: no tribute payments, return of the captured Americans and no future enslavement of American sailors. In return the Dey only got the return of the two captured ships and surviving members of their crews.

Later that summer Decatur completed his mission by forcing Tunis and Tripoli to pay reparations for American prizes they had seized during the War of 1812. In addition to cash payments from both, the Bashaw was forced by Decatur to turnover10 enslaved Europeans. Remembering who had befriended the Americans during their earlier war with Tripoli, Decatur selected Danes and Sicilians to free, in remembrance of the kindness of Nicholas Nissen to American captives, and the loan of Sicilian gunboats.

By the time of the arrival of Bainbridge's squadron, Decatur was done. Running to Gibraltar on Guerriere (unaccompanied), Decatur came upon seven Algerian warships, much of their remaining fleet.. Decatur prepared his ship for action, but the Algerians only posed a question---where was he going. Decatur's response spoke loudly of what he and the Navy had accomplished: "American ships sail where they please."

Bibliography

Adams, Henry, History of the United States during the Administrations of Thomas Jefferson and James Madison. 4 vols. New York: A&C Boni, 1930.

Allen, Gardner W. Our Navy and the Barbary Corsairs, Hampden, Conn.: Archon Books, 1905.

Allison, Robert J. The Crescent Obscured: The United States and the Muslim World, 1776-1815. New York, Oxford: Oxford University Press, 1995.

Barber, Noel. The Sultans. New York: Simon and Schuster, 1973.

Bradford, Ernie. The Sultan's Admiral: The Life of Barbarossa. New York: Harcourt, Brace & World, Inc., 1968.

Bridge, Anthony. Suleiman the Magnificent: Scourge of Heaven. New York: Franklin Watts, 1983.

Brodie, Fawn M. Thomas Jefferson: An Intimate History. New York: W.W. Norton & Co. Inc., 1974.

Canney, Daniel. Sailing Warships of the US Navy. Annapolis, Maryland: Naval Institute Press, 2001.

Edwards, Samuel. Barbary General: The Life of William H. Eaton. Englewood Cliffs, N.J.: Prentice-Hall, Inc., 1968.

Ellis, Joseph J. American Sphinx: The Character of Thomas Jefferson. New York: Alfred A. Knopf, 1997.

Fisher, Godrey. Barbary Legend: War, Trade and Piracy in North Africa. Oxford: Clarendon Press, 1957.

Flexner, James Thomas. George Washington and the New Nation (1783-1793). Boston and Toronto. Little, Brown and Company, 1969.

Flexner, James Thomas. George Washington: Anguish and Farewell. Boston, Toronto: Little, Brown and Company, 1969.

Forester, C.S. The Barbary Pirates. New York: Random House, 1953.

Fowler, William M., Jr. Jack Tars and Commodores: The American Navy 1783-1815. Boston: Houghton Mifflin and Company. 1984.

Franklin, Benjamin. Writings. New York: The Library of America. 1987.

Goodwin, Jason. Lord of the Horizons: A History of the Ottoman Empire. New York: Henry Holt and Company. 1998.

Gosse, Philip. The History of Piracy. New York: Tudor Publishing Company. 1995.

Howarth, Stephen. To Shining Sea: A History of the United States Navy 1775-1991. New York: Random House. 1991.

Jefferson, Thomas. Public and Private Papers. New York: First Vintage Books. 1990.

Jefferson, Thomas. The Papers of Thomas Jefferson, Volume 18. Princeton, N.J.: Princeton University Press. 1971.

Johnson, Paul. A History of the American People. New York: Harper Collins. 1997.

Kitzen, Michael L.S. Tripoli and the United States at War: A History of American Relations with the Barbary States 1785-1805. Jefferson, N.C., London: McFarland & Company, Inc. 1993.

Knox, Dudley W. A History of the United States Navy. New York: G.P. Putnam's Sons. 1936.

Knox, Dudley W. The Naval Genius of George Washington. Boston: Houghton Mifflin Company. 1932.

Lambert, Frank. The Barbary Wars: American Independence in the Atlantic World. New York: Hill and Wang. 2005.

Lehman, John. On Seas of Glory: Heroic Men, Great Ships and Epic Battles of the American Navy. New York: The Free Press. 2001.

The Life and Selected Writings of Thomas Jefferson. New York: The Modern Library, Edited by Adrienne Koch and William Peden.

Malone, Dumas. Jefferson and His Time, 6 vols. Boston: Little, Brown and Company. 1948.

Martin, Tyrone G. A Most Fortunate Ship: A Narrative History of Old Ironsides. Annapolis, Md.: Naval Institute Press, 1997.

McCullough, David. John Adams. New York: Simon & Schuster, 2001.

McKee, Christopher. Edward Preble, A Naval Biography, 1761-1807. Annapolis, Md.: Naval Institute Press, 1972.

Minnigerode, Meade. Lives and Times: Four Informal American Biographies (William Eaton, Hero). New York and London: G.P. Putnam's Sons, 1925.

Morison, Samuel Eliot. Oxford History of the American People. New York: Oxford University Press, 1965.

Naval Documents Related to the United States Wars with the Barbary Powers. 6 vols. Washington: US Government Printing Office, 1939.

Peterson, Merrill D. Thomas Jefferson and he New Navy. New York: Oxford University Press, 1970.

Piracy, Slavery and Redemption: Barbary Captivity Narratives from Early Modern England. New York: Columbia University Press. 2001. Edited by Daniel J. Vitkus.

Pratt, Fletcher. Preble's Boys: Commodore Preble and the Birth of American Sea Power. New York: William Sloane Associates, 1950.

Randall, William Sterne. Thomas Jefferson: A Life. New York: Henry Holt. 1993.

The Republic of Letters: The Correspondence between Thomas Jefferson and James Madison 1776-1826. 3 vols. New York and London: W.W. Norton & Company. 1995. Edited by James Morton Smith.

Robotti, Frances Diane, and Vescovi, James. The USS Essex and the Birth of the

American Navy. Holbrook, Massachusetts: Adams Media Corporation. 1999.

Toll, Ian W. Six Frigates: The Epic History of the Founding of the U.S. Navy. New York and London: W.W. Norton & Company, 2006.

Tucker, Glenn. Dawn Like Thunder: The Barbary Wars and the Birth of the U.S. Navy. Indianapolis: The Bobbs-Merrill Company, Inc., 1963.

Van Alstyne, Richard W. American Diplomacy in Action. Gloucester, Mass.: Peter Smith, 1968.

Walters, Raymond, Jr. Albert Gallatin: Jeffersonian Financier and Diplomat. New York: The MacMilllan Company, 1957.

Wheelan, Joseph. Jefferson's War: America's First War on Terror, 1801-1805. New York: Carroll & Graf, 2003.

White Slaves, African Masters. Chicago and London: University of Chicago Press, 1999. Edited by Paul Baepler.

Whipple, A.B.C. To the Shores of Tripoli: The Birth of the U.S. Navy and Marines. New York: William Morrow and Company, Inc., 1991.

Whittier, John Greenleaf. The Poetical Works of Whittier. Boston: Houghton Mifflin Company, 1975.

Wolf, John B. The Barbary Coast: Algeria Under the Turks 1500-1830. New York and London: W.W. Norton & Company, 1979.

The Works of John Adams, Second President of the United States. Vol. IX. Boston: Little, Brown and Company, 1854. Edited by Charles Francis Adams.

Wright, Louis B. and Macleod, Julia H. The First Americans in North Africa: William Eaton's Struggle for a Vigorous Policy against the Barbary Pirates, 1799-1805. Princeton, New Jersey: Princeton University Press, 1945.

The Writings of Thomas Jefferson, Vol. X. Washington: The Thomas Jefferson Memorial Association of the United States. 1904. Edited by Andrew A. Lipscomb and Albert Ellery Bergh.

The Writings of Thomas Jefferson: Being his Autobiography, Correspondence, Reports,

Messages, Addresses, and other Writings, Official and Private. Washington: Taylor & Maury, 1854.

Zacks, Richard. The Pirate Coast. New York: Hyperion Books. 2005.

Philip Blake worked as a newspaper reporter, general manager and publisher for 30 years before retiring in 2001. He started his career as a reporter for the City News Bureau of Chicago, and also was a city desk reporter at the Chicago Daily News in the early 1970's.

He served as a line officer in the US Navy from 1966 to 1969, including service as operations officer of a destroyer in the Mediterranean seas plied by the Barbary pirates 160 years earlier.

He received a B.A. degree in international relations from Brown University in 1966 and a Masters in management from Northwestern University in 1979.

He served as publisher of the Wisconsin State Journal from 1993 to 2000, and of The Missoulian from 1986 to 1993.

www.ingramcontent.com/pod-product-compliance
Lightning Source LLC
LaVergne TN
LVHW011408080426
835511LV00005B/439